Abundance

Abundance

Eating and living with the Seasons

Mark Diacono

Quadrille

CONTENTS

Opening word   9

January   12
February   40
March   56
April   78
May   102
June   120
July   140
August   164
September   184
October   210
November   236
December   260

Closing word   279

Index   280
Acknowledgements   284
About the author   284
An extra thank you   285

For everyone who followed Abundance as it happened and made it what it is

It was not unusual to find me two pints in of an afternoon[1] with (like any self-respecting teenager too scared of life to throw himself at the mercy of Kerouac's 'road') a Bukowski in hand. I was rarely one for poetry, and while almost everything of the inner pages has left my memory, the title – *The Days Run Away Like Wild Horses Over the Hills* – has stuck to me like goose shit to suede.

Here am I, what seems like a fortnight later, decades older.

Life is good. Unbelievably I found something I was meant to do, that scratches a creative itch I didn't know I had, that means I never have to squash myself into the world of working for someone else again. Others seem to like it well enough for me to do it ongoingly. I've become incrementally more content; increasingly appreciative of the everyday.

And yet there is a semi-distant itch.

I am neither young nor old: of an age where I might have 40 minutes or 40 years left before the big fella has me row to the side of the lake. Despite things being good, I have a sense of watching my life's movie in a virtual cinema, at a distance from me. I'm now impatient to live those minutes or years more fully; to be more *in* them.

Almost as soon as I recognised this desire, the idea for how I might go about it came when I woke early one chilly day with the idea for *Abundance* fully formed in my sleepy head.

That word – abundance – glowing in my mind like a childhood ice-cream van catching the late afternoon sun. It captured everything I had yet hoped to feel more connected to in this life of growing, cooking, walking and writing. I would write every week about what I pick from my garden, the recipes I cook, the landscapes in which I live, life's small pleasures… and whatever else sprung from the soil and sea of this patch of South West England.

I hadn't the faintest idea if it would work, but it immediately felt right; like taking the time to write down a year of my life, week by week, might not only place me more wholly in 'life' but maybe also slow the speedy passing of those wild horses through the rearview mirror.

---

1 Jeez, how good is the world lived two pints in?

Windscreen wipers, Big Al, the Grand Canyon and the best porridge

I am the only one awake. Even the dog snores, oblivious. I light the morning fire from the final crackle of last night's locked-down blaze: a simple, deep pleasure.

The kettle – a stovetop whistler – makes a slow ladder of steam to the ceiling. The initial sip of the first coffee of the morning is good: a small, crucial joy in someone else's kitchen.

Before long, the old stairs will crack to the weight of sleepy feet in search of breakfast. I make the porridge; (a sleeping) Big Al's water method yields something more luscious than it has any right to, but my love of creaminess endures. I make a small concession to his brilliance by soaking the oats in boiling water to start.[1]

The first day of the year. It's good to be away from home. Distance nourishes my mind's ability to contemplate life in the abstract, to ponder a few intentions (if not quite resolutions) without the need to put them in place right this minute, today.

The first coffee of the year windscreen wipes what went before. What will this new year bring? I am old enough that the hope that everyone I love is here in 365 days is relevant enough to need expressing. The urge to live better, more fully, more attentively, if not so much in the present then the very recent past, is strong.

I intend to spend the year writing about the year itself, whatever it brings, knowing the undercurrent will be what I grow, forage, harvest and cook. Beyond that, who knows?

I hope that writing every week will give me the excuse to be more attentive to whatever has its moment that day, to be more embedded in the shifts of each week, and to feel carried by the tide of the seasons.

I hope it will make me feel more alive, attached more elementally to the everything, to live to the truth of what we all know – that we are temporarily agglomerated atoms on a rock spinning through space and that it'll soon be over – rather than the illusion of immortality

---

1 I'm not sure there's a greater compliment someone can give than to amend their porridge method to recognise the excellence of someone else's.

that we place in front of our eyes every morning in the hope of distancing the enormity of our pointlessness. Pointless or not, I want to be undistracted from the sweet pleasures of this gorgeous life, to discover and revel in more of them by burrowing a little more deeply into the everyday miracles that surround us.

That I live in a part of the planet that constantly changes, that brings four utterly contrasting seasons, and with them a rolling menu of deliciousness, is a life-enhancing joy not lost on me.

I want to make the most of it. I intend to soak it all up; not by abseiling down the Eiffel Tower, hand-gliding through the Grand Canyon or getting out of my mind on a bucketload of exhilarants, but by immersing myself more fully in the what, why and now of where I am. I don't want more length, I want more depth. I don't really want more than that right now.

The thud of two feet, then four on the floor above. Time to light the candles, fan the fire and lay the table.

New Year porridge

Anyone can make porridge, but can you *make* porridge? Like makin' lurve and parallel parking, people are often reluctant to receive instruction from someone who is confident in their mastery of a thing people like to think they are already familiar with. Immodest as it may be, I am happy to extend the benefit of excellence in (sadly only) two of these areas, one of them being porridge.

Texture is as important as flavour here: this method of adding the oats in two stages gets you gloss with bite; the lack of sugar in the porridge itself lets the nuts, cream, jelly and syrup do the sweetening work. I used to think it had to be demerara sugar, but once you use excellent maple syrup there is no going back.

I used Flahavan's organic oats (the best and they are not too large) along with oat milk for a deeper oat flavour.

SERVES 4

180g (6oz) rolled oats
360ml (12fl oz) oat milk
25g (1oz) lightly crushed nuts (I used walnuts)
25g (1oz) lightly crushed seeds (I used half sunflower, half pumpkin)
double (heavy) cream
maple syrup or mugolio (page 103)
jam or jelly (try the jelly on page 275)
sea salt

Stir 300ml (10fl oz) boiling water into a pan containing 100g (3½oz) of the oats. Allow it to rest for 5 minutes.

Place over a low-medium heat and bring to a simmer. Add a very good pinch of salt.

Stir in the oat milk and return to a simmer. Add the rest of the oats, stirring frequently to prevent them sticking to the bottom of the pan. Allow the porridge to come back to a simmer and cook for 2–3 minutes at most, adding a touch more milk if you need to get to something a little more mobile than a dropping consistency.

Spoon into bowls, dash with nuts and seeds, then slick with cream followed by maple syrup and a dollop of jam.

Three-cornered leeks, a hoppy ale, a chef called Tim and a double yolker

These early New Year days have me wanting to be out early, walking, ideally by the sea, returning to eat too much in excellent company, a good hoppy ale by the fire while collecting strands of bath-thoughts and mini revelations into a rope of aims and resolutions for the year ahead.

I managed most of that but somehow it's the 10th and the last part evades me. The plans I used to make in the days between unwrapping and the turn of the year get pushed back a little more every January.

My intentions for the year feel like a sneeze that orbits as a faint tickle without quite landing. It feels similar to being on the home straight of writing a book, where there's no telling when it'll be finished: it genuinely might be in 15 minutes or the week after next.

Despite decades of experience, New Year's Day still feels – as I wrote in *A Year at Otter Farm* – like 'I've pedalled over winter's hill and that it'll be a freewheel into spring. Of course it isn't – January will seem two optimistic weeks long and February like a month and a half of icy winds – but at least for the early part of January, I'm happy.'

This morning, while the positivity is still here, I planned a day of scribbling in the hope of resolving and envisaging. I transferred a pile of notes and wrapping paper jottings to a single page in the hope they'd form a personal and professional recipe for the year – if I pushed them around the page's plate long enough.

Instead, drawn by the sun and too long not seeing my mum – and despite a sense of urgency about deadlines to meet – I pushed everything to one side and took the long way round to meet her for excellent coffee and, yes, morning cake.

Along the river and in great swathes around the leafless trees, lush gonks of what look from a distance like flowerless daffodils: it is three-cornered leek.[1] Far ahead of the wild garlic, it makes its optimistic way into the new year light, the first wild harvest of the season.

---

1 Aka Snowbell, *Allium triquetrum*.

It is easy to distinguish from other seemingly similar plants: in profile, the leaves form a shallow V-shape, the flower stems a three-pronged star, and the scent is a mild yet very present leekiness with a hint of distant garlic.

The river path is bound by one of those diamond-wired fences of the sort that made the sides of the football cage at every school in the '80s; I leant over it and cut a couple of handfuls of three-cornered leeks[2] that were beyond the peeing range of all but perhaps the tallest and most generously blessed of the neighbourhood hounds. I popped them in my bag, the cut ends saved from too much evaporation by a solo poo bag lurking in my coat pocket. Coffee with my mum may have had her wondering – but not asking – what the peculiar oniony scent was.

I made plans for the three-cornered leeks on the way home – adjika perhaps, pesto at a push, maybe an oil to go with that leek and potato soup I plan on making – but in the end, after a little soaking to wash off any undesirables, I did the simple, obvious and most pleasurable thing: I softened them in butter before slowly scrambling what was meant to be three but – courtesy of the last being a double yolker – became four eggs. A good deal of salt, a heavy peppering and a tweak of chilli flakes and the work of a few minutes became the best lunch. My wife ate it with excellent rye bread toast.

Simplicity. It also reminded me of old friend and brilliant chef Tim Maddams, who introduced me to eating three-cornered leek one cold winter eight years ago; a man who showed up when times were not great, and who lives with boldness, courage and originality. He griddled the late-season stems – flowers, bulbs and all – made a lively romesco sauce to go with, and it lit up an extraordinary meal he made for twenty-odd. I'll go back later in the year to harvest more when the six-petalled, green-striped white flowers are hanging and ferment some and griddle plenty to eat with Tim's romesco.

I've just written down a few of the words that leapt off these last couple of pages:

> simplicity / see mum / cook for people you love / be outside when the sun shines / take the long way round / boldness and courage / cake

Crystallising those resolutions might come sooner than expected.

---

2 Three-cornered leek might not be the most common plant in the world, but where it does establish it does so with enthusiasm, so you can harvest with reasonable certainty that you are not likely to make a dent in its existence. Here in the UK, it is an offence to plant the bulbs in the wild.

Micro-seasons, Baden-Powell, a Galaxy Ripple and a perfect January soup

The traditional Japanese calendar has 72 *kō* micro seasons to the year; windows of 5 or so days characterised by the coming together of particular phenomena – bud burst of this; that bird arriving – with rituals, celebrations, foods coming into season and more. I love that idea. Today, the day seemed noticeably longer than the close of last week, the skies a little fuller of birdsong; something beyond weather. It draws to a close the *kō* characterised by the words 'springs once frozen flow once more'.

The passing of a man through middle age might well be comprised of a similar number of micro-seasons of loss of dignity: when trying on your new shorts you stare into the mirror and Baden-Powell stares back; a few years later, you wear a coat of which you are unsure of the shade or style but you rejoice in its warmth, and suddenly warmth is *enough*. For me, today is that day.

Needing a leg-stretch in a place likely without people, I took to the hill to the east of town. Stepping out from the trees, the wind hit me in the face like a cold carrier bag, my body luxuriantly impervious to it. I felt a deep smugness, of the kind ordinarily reserved for something as monumental as casting a scrunched-up wrapper into the bin, from distance, with a pleasing clank.

It became a walk defined by the carry of a woodpecker's busy head-butting. I left the car to the 20-donks-a-second sound of his distant work, a sound that reminds me of childhood cartoon-running sound effects. Being in the company of a woodpecker will never not make me happy.

It is to this hill I come in spring for gorse flowers, coconutty in scent and flavour, to infuse in rum, sugar syrup and more (page 105). It does pretty well on these high peaks of red-brown mudstones, uncoincidentally of the same colour as the bricks that make so many of the houses down the slope.

I head to the sea, a cliff fall – the path now many metres below – causing me to take a different turn along the coast. We take to the field where the dog is driven half-crazy by a family of rabbits long-gone to the warren, who've scattered their poo like Maltesers,

Revels and Treets across the field. He runs between them as if he were a baseball home-runner, lost to the joy of the very best his culinary world has to offer.

We make slow poo-eating progress to the edge of the dip to the valley, where I'm greeted by a Jaffa cake sunrise. The sea is as smooth as the surface of a Galaxy Ripple.

A rash of wishes for the days ahead fills my brain. One early summer day, when the light beats people's alarm, I want to lay on a paddleboard in the shallows just off that beach on a morning as still as this. In late spring, I'll walk to that Dorset field of flowering broad beans – still the most intoxicating scent I've ever smelt. And perhaps this will be the year I make it to the mindfulness centre Plum Village… I utter a quiet promise to myself and my still-sleeping wife to soon come to the beach below, frying pan in hand, to make a fire and breakfast before the sun rises.

Retracing my steps, a robin hops out of invisibility on to skeletal blackthorn. A friend wherever they appear. I'm not sure how much I believe that they are the feathery representation of someone who has died come to visit, but I know it gives my mum much comfort and I do hope it's true.

As we leave the field of (rabbit poo) dreams, a clutch of nine young house sparrows lifts from the hedge, briefly forming a moving Cassiopeia against the blue sky as they flitter up the valley, and I follow them home, the woodpecker still knocking its way into the day.

Tomorrow starts the *kō*:

Kiji hajimete naku
Cock pheasants begin to call

I shall keep an ear out.

Cauliflower and sage soup

Sage and cauliflower are such a great pairing that suits these slow, lengthening days: hope and comfort in a bowl. If ever there was a case for white pepper, this is it. It rises on the steam of the soup to inhabit your nostrils in a cloud of pleasure. Buy white peppercorns and grind them yourself; it makes such a difference here.

SERVES 6–8

2 tsp coriander seeds
2 tsp cumin seeds
1 tbsp butter
1 tbsp olive oil, plus more for the sage
2 onions, finely chopped
2 garlic cloves, finely chopped
1 medium-large cauliflower, chopped into 3cm (1in) cubes
1.2 litres (2 pints) hot water
12 sage leaves
curry powder, to serve
sea salt and freshly ground white pepper

Toast the coriander and cumin in a dry pan set over a medium heat until they become fragrant, agitating the pan to prevent burning. Reduce to a coarse powder using a mortar and pestle or spice grinder.

Warm the butter and oil in a large pan over a medium heat. Reduce the heat and add the onions and a good pinch of salt. Cook, stirring, for 15 minutes or so until translucent and soft. Add the garlic and the ground toasted spices and stir well. Add the cauliflower and the water, then bring to the boil. Reduce the heat and simmer for 12–15 minutes until the cauliflower is cooked but firm. Remove from the heat and blend (in batches if needs be) until smooth. Keep the soup warm, seasoning to taste with salt and white pepper.

Add just enough olive oil to a small frying pan to reach a depth of 3mm (⅛in). Warm it over a medium heat, then carefully add the sage leaves (in batches to avoid crowding the pan) and fry until crisp and lightly coloured. Lift out and transfer to a plate lined with kitchen paper.

Ladle the soup into bowls, sprinkle with a little curry powder and white pepper, dot with fried sage leaves, and swirl with the sage-infused olive oil.

Seville oranges, allspice, a wintry mojito and Joan Collins

January is the month I make marmalade for other people. While my love for Seville orange marmalade is deep, it is infrequent: if I make 12 jars, I keep only 2.

I often make Seville orange and cardamom gin, or a very special Seville orange curd[1] – any new arrivals on this thinnest part of the seasonal conveyor belt should be celebrated, after all – but this year I resolved to think of a new recipe before I bought any.

Breakfast: Marmite on toast. It finished the jar.

I looked up from checking emails while I ate to see a tray of unpromising nuggets: dandelion roots that my wife had exhumed, washed and chopped. My wife is a medical herbalist with years of training and experience. She has been telling me – in short instalments as she knows I'm hard of thinking – about dandelion's properties, its benefits to digestion and gut health. What she hadn't told me was why the perfect place for these roots to dry was, apparently, on the shelf above my computer screen.

Adding a jar of Marmite to the shopping list tipped the scales towards a supermarket visit. I was met by a wall of Seville oranges. My resolve dissolved: I bought a net of 10.

The Seville orange gin I make has much to recommend it – gently bitter and lively as it is – but a few months ago, with the last sip of the last batch, a small bell rang in my mind: would this be good if it was intensified, if everything was turned up a few notches, to become a bitters?

My January brain picked up that autumn thread.

A bitters is a drink traditionally made by infusing alcohol with big flavours – usually including herbs and/or spices – that lend it a bitter or bittersweet flavour. You might be familiar with angostura bitters, or Campari.[2] Orange bitters is a much-loved variation on the bitters theme.

1 Both recipes appear in my book *Sour*.
2 Joan Collins and Leonard Rossiter's TV adverts did much to make Campari a popular drink in the 1970s.

I told my wife my excellent Seville orange plan. 'And by the way, what's happening with those dandelion roots above my desk?'

'You should try some of the dried dandelion root in that bitters recipe.' She replied.

So, rather than make 1 litre, I've split the bitters into two half-litre jars, where the only difference is that one includes dandelion root, in order to give myself chance to see what effect it has.

Seville orange bitters

I spent my childhood summers in Lancashire, happily drowning in a sea of dandelion and burdock (then not available in the south). Its flavour is a cross between Coke, bay leaves and something that tastes purple, as odd as that sounds. I am as confident as I can be that it must be one (or both) of the ingredients in its name that made it so special. I'm hoping it's the dandelion.

As I start making it, I have an old memory of being told not to play with – and most certainly do not eat – dandelions, as they will make you pee yourself. It turns out that their old English folk name is 'piss-a-bed' (the French have an equivalent) in response to the apparently diuretic effect of the plant's roots. Given that the recipe involves a good deal of vodka I'm not going to worry about a bit of dandelion.

Seville oranges do a working men's club impersonation of other oranges. Rather than tight and juicy, they are as slack as end-of-year school tennis balls, so use the sharpest peeler you have.

MAKES TWO 500ML (18FL OZ) JARS

10 Seville oranges
½ tbsp coriander seeds
½ tbsp fennel seeds
8 cardamom pods, gently crushed
2 handfuls of dried dandelion root (optional)
1 litre (1¾ pints) vodka

Preheat the oven to 140°C/120°C fan/285°F.

Use a peeler to remove the zest of the oranges, then spread the zest on a baking sheet. Place in the centre of the oven for 40 minutes, shaking it once in a while. The zest strips needn't be entirely desiccated but they should smell lively and be fairly dry; allow a little extra time if needed.

Add the spices, the dried zest and the dandelion root (if using) to a jar (or jars) large enough to hold all the ingredients, then pour over the vodka. Stir and cover.

Allow to infuse, out of direct sunlight, for 2 weeks, shaking every day or so.

A week later

Both bitters are very orangey and bitterly delicious. The difference is marked: the one with the dandelion root – maybe like a smoky whisky – takes a little more getting to know as the bitterness is distinctly upped, though so is the complexity.

How will I use them? I think the dandelion bitters might be the more 'medicinal' – for post- and pre-meal digestifs – while the other might be more 'recreational', taking over the Campari duties in negronis and to enjoy with soda.

As it turns out, I got two recipes from those 10 fruit.

The bitters recipe uses just the zest, and it seemed a shame to offer all that fruit to the compost without using its flavour first.

A text came in from a friend: we should go for a post-Christmas catch-up, he suggested. Of the many things that flash across my mind when I think of him is his love of spiced rum.

Another lightbulb.

This is so often how – if you can relax enough to let it happen – recipes walk out of the mist towards you.

Seville orange spiced rum

Here bitterness, sourness and spices dominate, while leaving me room to sweeten depending on how I plan to drink it. You'll find spiced rum recipes with vanilla pods, cinnamon and other spices that imply sweetness: I've gone for allspice, largely because its characteristics are perfect here but also as it shares a Caribbean home with rum. It's exceptional with plenty of ice, ginger beer and a little nutmeg syrup, fig leaf syrup or the syrup from a jar of stem ginger. But perhaps the best way to use it is in a wintry mojito.

MAKES 700ML (1¼ PINTS)

the flesh (pith and zest removed) of 10 Seville oranges
8 allspice berries, lightly crushed
a monkey's paw of ginger, peeled and thinly sliced
700ml (1¼ pints) white rum

Squeeze each orange into a large Kilner jar and add the allspice and ginger. Pour the rum into the jar and leave for a week before tasting; leave longer if you fancy, or strain and decant into a bottle. Enjoy as it is, or with ginger beer and plenty of ice.

Seville orange wintry mojito

The classic mojito – white rum, lime, mint, sugar and soda water – is open to endless variations, and as a seasonal new year uplifter this one is hard to beat. Take this as a guide and taste and adjust as you like. This is very gingery: you can ease it back by going for ginger ale rather than ginger beer, or swap for soda or tonic water for something very different.

SERVES 1

small handful of mint
ice
2 tbsp Seville orange spiced rum (see recipe above)
2 tbsp syrup from a jar of stem ginger
ginger beer

Slap the mint between your hands to encourage the scent and flavour to release. Add the ice, slapped mint, rum and syrup to a tallish glass, then add a couple of inches of ginger beer, taste and adjust as you wish. Enjoy on a cold winter's day, the sun shining through the window, while enjoying the benefit of central heating.

Albert Camus, fat balls, *The Truman Show* and a stupendous flapjack

The wind is cold and from nowhere comes a craving for flapjack. I stare at the garden and have no urge to be in it. Judging by its diminishing stock,[1] the birds are clearly enjoying the bird feeder, but even they can't be arsed at the moment. Other than a lardass of a pigeon failing to balance on the top, I've seen a house finch; that's it.

The ridiculousness of gardening has filled my mind for a few days. Shouldn't I dedicate those weekends and evenings not to tending a peculiar creation but to walking the coast path, striding the fells, or lowering this unpleasant frame into a loch or lake? Aren't there plenty of places on this beautiful spinning rock yet to amaze me? And yet I waste my time a few feet away.

Are we, I wonder, players in a Truman Show of our own making, pulling in the boundary ropes of our own existence, using screens to take us elsewhere, creating gardens to keep us from exploring the planet – whatever it takes to distract us from our mortality and, as a consequence, prevent us being more fully, truly alive.

We are, as Joni so perfectly put it, 'only particles of change, orbiting around the sun';[2] walking compost, worm food in waiting, atoms temporarily agglomerated in what we hope is a package attractive enough to distract someone from their Sudoku long enough to jump on us in pleasure once in a while.

Whenever I play Joni's 'Hejira' – a perfect love song to travelling and the search for whatever – I realise I should be elsewhere; living that truly whole life and all the experiences it has to offer before the unseeable view lays before my eyes.

Albert Camus wrote that when we travel we are looking for a fresh, deep connection to the eternal: 'At that moment we are feverish but also porous, so that the slightest touch makes us quiver to the depths of our being. We come across a cascade of light, and there is eternity'.[3] As a man striding through the middle years of his life with little idea of whether

---

1 See how I resisted the temptation to make any 'fat balls' jokes.
2 From her perfect album *Hejira*.
3 There's no doubt Joni was reading Camus' *Notebooks, 1935–1942 (Volume 1)*, from which that quote was taken, around this time, given her lyrics to 'Hejira'.

he will rupture something crucial courtesy of an ill-timed sneeze, that cascade of light sure sounds more appealing than once again refilling the green bin.

And yet I can't quite let it, the garden, go.

There is a theory that rather than us having domesticated the apple, it domesticated us. Bribed by the deliciousness of its fresh and fermented fruit, we did its work, spreading its genetic material far and wide, adjusting its character to better suit us and more effectively facilitate its global colonisation. Every winter, when the wind comes and I wrestle with the point of gardening, I wonder whether we are not similarly domesticated: upright woodlice, here to build topsoil on which higher organisms (worms, soil micro-organisms and the rest) might thrive. Is this urge to garden perhaps a higher calling, drawn to a close by surrendering our temporary agglomeration to its one true purpose?

As I write this, the sunrise catches the soft slopes of the Sid valley, picking out the gentle green of permanent pasture, a solid line above which a mix of conifer tangles with the deciduous. I should walk it more, but it occurs to me that all of that middle distance is an interpretation of the opportunities and constraints of the geology, soil and topography. It is a cultural painting of how we scratch an existence from what circumstance dealt our little corner of the planet. On this peculiar island, almost nothing is natural in its truest sense – a scrap of the Cairngorms, the uppermost Walnut Whip of a highland peak, perhaps – the rest is what (for good or ill) we have made of it. Whether by tractor, chainsaw or rake, almost all of it is gardening of one kind or another.

And as much as Joni's 'Hejira' is about travel, it is about how travel lights the flames of home a little warmer, and how neither way is the golden ticket: 'You know it never has been easy, Whether you do or you do not resign, Whether you travel the breadth of extremities, Or stick to some straighter line'. Travel, or don't: it's all here, right now, if we pay attention.

I turn it up, open fresh seed packets and sow chillies, tomatoes and aubergines in hope as much as expectation. I thank my lucky stars that the shift from unsettled, directionless, troubled man to purposeful, creative, grateful soul began the moment – the actual instant – that I grew a little of what I ate for the first time.

Cranberry and caraway flapjack

As with 'The Whole of the Moon' by The Waterboys,[4] I have the urge for flapjack once in a long while, and when I do, nothing else will suffice. This is on the softer side: if you like it crunchier, up the temperature by 10°C (50°F) and/or cook it a little longer, or use a slightly larger dish and its thinness will make it crisper.

You might be raising an eyebrow at the caraway – I promise you it is a delight, even without the other flavours, but the joyful sour tweak of the nose provided by cranberries and lemon is elevated by caraway's weird minty-earthiness (a quality I think only it and shiso have), which in turn is elevated further when enjoyed with excellent coffee.

MAKES 16 LAUGHABLY SMALL PIECES OF WHICH YOU WILL HAVE TWO, SO CUT IT INTO 8

300g (10½oz) butter
65g (2¼oz) demerara sugar
65g (2¼oz) golden syrup
65g (2¼oz) honey
450g (1lb) rolled oats
100g (3½oz) dried cranberries, roughly chopped
½ tbsp caraway seeds
zest of 1 lemon
good pinch of salt

Preheat the oven to 195°C/175°C fan/350°F. Line a 24cm (9in) square dish or baking tin with baking parchment (or grease well with butter and take your chances).

In a medium pan set over a low-medium heat, melt the butter, sugar and honey together, stirring often. In a large bowl, mix together the oats, cranberries, caraway, lemon zest and salt, then pour over the sweet melted butter and stir until fully combined.

Spoon into the dish and use the back of the spoon to press the mixture into the edges and corners.

Bake in the centre of the oven for 25 minutes, or until lightly golden. As soon as you remove it from the oven, use a sharp knife to cut it into squares (or greedy rectangles), then allow to cool completely and firm up in the dish before removing.

4 I had the very great pleasure of falling out of the back of a van into Dublin at Christmas in the late '80s and seeing The Waterboys at the height of their powers. A few years later I saw Mike Scott (the singer) solo in a church in Salisbury. Both times 'The Whole of the Moon' shone saccharin-free and glorious, away from adverts and mini-series misplacement. One day, ideally in a West Coast bar, I shall hear it again.

Sherlock Holmes, a superb stew, John Martyn and the unpleasantness of pigeons

It's 6.55 a.m.

I often wake at this time. The old man set his alarm for 6.55 – its tinny clang floating across the landing to scrape at my ears. Five minutes later, kettle on, radio on, he'd be stood in the lav, door half open, farting in time with the 7 a.m. pips.

This morning, this early, the garden, the street, the town, is flooded in a Sherlock Holmes fog: everything is damp; there's no space where space normally is. It's the kind of day it's hard to find a reason to leave the house, but if you don't it can feel like you're back in bed before you've got up.

I'm going nowhere, though. Not even to the shops. Today is best served by cooking, a fire, John Martyn in my ears and a short nose around the garden. Between them, the veg patch, the fridge and the cupboard are going to have to provide.

I have a friend a few miles up the coast who has one rule about growing food: he's not giving up space to anything that takes as long to arrive as a baby. No sprouts, give over celery, not interested in cauliflower, and so on. It's a good rule if you have limited space: why dedicate even a square foot for most of a year for the reward of just one meal? The downside is that as lively and abundant as the ten warmest months of the year are when you prioritise them, these early weeks are the leanest. But there is something; there is always something.

And today's something is chard. We grow a few varieties, including the colourful Bright Lights and the white-ribbed Fordhook Giant. Not content with taking up residence in the wisteria and shagging their way through spring, the pigeons seem inclined towards the Fordhook Giant at this time of year, but leave the Bright Lights mercifully untouched.

Cutting the stems a couple of inches from the soil leaves the plant with enough of an engine room to resprout for harvesting again in a couple of summer weeks, and maybe three or four times that at this sluggish point in the year.

The spells of endless rain have left the chard in need of a soak – the soil beneath splashed on to the leaves and into the grooves of the stalks – but half an hour soaking in the sink and they're clean, leaving a powdery tea around the plughole.

The fridge offers up a head of celery, a lemon and a half handful of tarragon. The celery has as much flavour as the day it was picked, and a lemon can save almost anything.

In the end, I got two delicious recipes out of everything – cooked and prepared in the time it took *Solid Air* to bring a little sunshine to this foggy day.

Chard, celery, butter bean and tarragon stew with celery and tarragon pesto

This stew was just what we needed.

I make a version of this with twice the celery but no chard, and cream instead of coconut milk, but I have a feeling it could bend to any time of year and any mood: a sea of root vegetables and some kale; tomatoes for half the celery and basil pesto, and so on.

A glass of cider instead of the stock works brilliantly here – apples and tarragon are very good friends – and a glass to go with wouldn't harm either.

SERVES 6

3 tbsp olive oil, plus a little to drizzle
1 head of celery (save the leaves and tender centre for the pesto, overleaf), sliced into 3cm (1in) pieces
2 onions, thinly sliced
2 bay leaves, cracked
400g (14oz) chard, stems thinly sliced, leaves roughly chopped
6 garlic cloves, finely chopped
150ml (5fl oz) vegetable stock, or water
400ml (14fl oz) can coconut milk
10g (½oz) tarragon
2 x 400g (14oz) cans butter beans, drained and rinsed
juice of ½ lemon
sea salt and freshly ground black pepper
celery and tarragon pesto (overleaf)
nutmeg, a good scratching

Heat the oil in a large, heavy-based pan over a low-medium heat and cook the celery and onions for 15 minutes, stirring often, until softened. Add the bay, chard stems and garlic and cook for a minute or two.

Add the stock, coconut milk, tarragon, a big pinch of salt and heavy grinding of pepper, cover and simmer gently, over a low-medium heat, for 25–30 minutes until tender.

Add the beans and chard leaves and simmer for 5 minutes. Add the lemon juice and adjust the seasoning if needed.

Serve with a good spoonful of celery pesto, a generous scratch of nutmeg, and – if you are thinking dinner rather than lunch – mashed potato and perhaps barely cooked tenderstem.

Celery and tarragon pesto

This is an extraordinarily good pesto that works as well with roasted anything as it does with the recipe above. And, of course, it is superb with pasta, though you might want to let it down with a touch more oil for that.

Don't be afraid to tweak this a little: the relative dryness of the almonds, the potency of the tarragon, the juiciness of the lemon and the bitterness of the oil can all impact the balance of flavours. A little water or extra oil might give you a consistency you prefer. If you eat cheese, a little grated Parmesan might make you happy, but I prefer it without.

MAKES A MEDIUM-SIZED JAR

leaves and tender centre from a head of celery – 80g (3oz) or so
55g (2oz) almonds
2 garlic cloves
4 good stems of tarragon, leaves only
finely grated zest of 1 lemon
juice of ½ lemon
6 tbsp olive oil
sea salt

Roughly chop the celery, almonds, garlic and tarragon and whizz together with all the remaining ingredients until almost smooth: I use a stick blender. Taste and adjust the seasoning to suit.

Forced rhubarb, three testicles, a Walnut Whip and an excellent cake

In a northern shed – right now, in the warm, in the dark – rhubarb is squeaking like stolen shoes.

In an unlikely fluke, some bright 19th-century spark recognised that their few square miles of Yorkshire enjoyed the perfect coming together of rain, soil and the waste wool, ashes and soot from local industry for growing rhubarb.

Perhaps the same lively mind also devised the method for producing the earliest, sweetest rhubarb that has made this triangle of Yorkshire so famous. When dormant in winter, rhubarb plants are lifted and brought into warm sheds. Fooled by the heat into thinking it's spring but denied the sunlight to photosynthesise, the plants convert their starch reserves into 'now' energy (sugar) and grow to meet the impostor season. Sweet, pale pink stems with yellow leaves result. And very fine they are too.

My rhubarb shows no sign of squeaking. Growing slow and steady even in this peculiarly mild late winter, it will be a while yet until I can pull a few fat, taut, crimson stems.

Next February, my plants will be established enough that I can replicate those northern sheds by placing a rhubarb forcer[1] over a couple of crowns; if idleness doesn't get the better of me, I might even shovel manure around them to further lift the temperature and give me sweet, vivid stems a month or more ahead of even the earliest unforced varieties. The downside is that after harvesting these forced stems, you have to allow the plant to recover for the rest of the year.

At our last home, we'd do this most years and my daughter – a rhubarb-lover to rival her dad – would help us pick it after school. I'd lift the heavy terracotta forcer off for her to get in there low with the perfect twisting technique that leaves the heart of the plant undamaged.

---

1 A tall terracotta impersonation of a Walnut Whip.

Soon, she'll have flown the nest, but I'm hoping I can tempt her back for a well-timed weekend of forced rhubarb picking and making this cake again, which she's just helped demolish. If not, I shall have to buy a box of Walnut Whips and hope that works instead.

Until then, I'm buying forced rhubarb and waiting for the equally and differently delicious unforced stalks to emerge.

Ginger and allspice olive oil cake with double ginger rhubarb

I make various versions of this deliciously nutty, moist, flourless cake, depending on mood and time of year. This is the core recipe, to which I might add a few quartered plums or peaches in summer. Today, I made it with a cake tin that was 23cm (9in) across, as I wanted a wider helipad on which to land the rhubarb; it gave a shallower cake that took 35 minutes to cook. Make a friend of this recipe and you'll return to it often, making it your own with different spices and fruit, in or on.

By all means serve this in slices with a jug of cream, but if you fancy a pud for everyone to dive into, as I did, pile the rhubarb on to the cake, spoon over the cooking syrup and anoint generously with double cream.

SERVES 8

120g (4oz) olive oil
120g (4oz) caster (superfine) sugar
3 eggs
200g (7oz) rolled oats, blitzed in a processor to a coarse powder
50g (2oz) ground almonds
1½ tsp ground allspice
1½ tsp baking powder
3 testicles of stem ginger, chopped
double ginger rhubarb (overleaf)
double (heavy) cream, to serve

Preheat the oven to 180°C/160°C fan/350°F and line the base of a deep, loose-based 20cm (8in) round cake tin with baking parchment.

Whisk the oil and sugar together thoroughly, then whisk in the eggs.

In another bowl, mix together the oat flour, ground almonds, allspice and baking powder, then stir this into the wet mixture, along with the stem ginger, until full incorporated. Pour into the cake tin.

Bake for 50 minutes, then test with a cocktail stick or cake tester: it will come out clean when ready.

Allow the cake to cool a little before running a knife around the edge of the cake and releasing it (with the base) from the tin. Set the cake on a lipped plate, pile on the double ginger rhubarb (below) and drizzle generously with cream to serve.

Double ginger rhubarb

You can cook this in the oven if it's already on, but with a cake in there that I didn't want to disturb I used the hob. As good a breakfast with yoghurt as there is, you can even whizz this up in a blender (having removed the rosemary) and make a bellini with one part ginger rhubarb to four of sparkling wine.

MAKES PLENTY FOR THE CAKE RECIPE ABOVE

400g (14oz) rhubarb, cut into 5cm (2in) lengths
3 tbsp syrup from a jar of stem ginger
3 sprigs of rosemary (ginger rosemary if you have it)

Place everything in a pan large enough that the rhubarb is in a single-ish layer. Add just enough water to cover the base and bring to a bare simmer. You want to catch this when it is just-cooked but still holds its shape: if the rhubarb is early and forced, it will take just a couple of minutes, perhaps 5–8 minutes for main-season rhubarb.

Remove from the pan as soon as it's tender and store in the fridge if not using immediately.

An unbroken chain, Nigel Slater, 93 million miles and a special coleslaw

The sun splashed across the dining table like spilt custard yesterday morning, and for a sweet moment I felt whole.

My skin sang, my mood lifted, my shoulders dropped. A shaft of light sent 8 minutes 20 seconds ago from 93 million miles away caught me unknowingly in need of exactly that; the complex individual that woke up too early rendered a clapping seal by nothing as unusual as a ray of welcome sunshine.

There's a song by Animal Collective that moves gradually from glorious semi-chaos into glorious sunshine.[1] Yesterday, as the sun bleached the table, felt exactly like that sounds. It has been endlessly grey, heavy with mist and cloudy: 'Grays where that color should be', as that song goes. Today and the rest of the week looks the same. I don't care. Yesterday came the antidote, imbuing me with the antibodies to handle it all.

An old friend too long unseen got on to the same train, into the same carriage, and the 10 morning minutes we shared between his boarding and my alighting were soaked in laughter and flashing sunshine. Soon after, I walked with another old friend who once again marvelled me with his inventive take on how to spend his time on this planet.[2] Later still, I stepped into the garden to talk to yet *another* good friend about an exciting opportunity that had fallen into his path, and having stepped into the garden saw light blasting shadows across and through what was in its path.

The artichokes with new lush growth next to desiccated flower stems that bore such deliciousness last summer; the Babington's leek (a perennial that thrives in the early part of the year) poking enthusiastically skywards.

---

1 'What Would I Want? Sky'. The glorious change happens from 2 minutes and 22 seconds. It features the first (and possibly only) Grateful Dead sample (from their song 'Unbroken Chain'). And what a gloriously inventive restitching they made of the original snippet.
2 In this case: minimise your outgoings, throw metaphorical hands into the soil and bring history into the light, explore how eating only whole grains, pulses and fresh vegetables might affect your physical and emotional system.

And when I came indoors, sitting waiting for the kettle to whistle, I accidentally discovered perhaps the best way to eat forced rhubarb – raw, dipped in the syrup that bathes golden orbs of jarred stem ginger.[3] It really is something else.

These are the days that not only put fuel in your tank, they oil the engine and every moving part.

Let it rain: everything is ok.

Fennel, rhubarb and radish coleslaw with elderflower dressing

Next time someone asks what you'd like for a birthday or Christmas, don't tell them not to bother or to get you something dull: tell them to get you a microplane. Kitchen life will thenceforth be divided into pre and post microplane.

This crisp, lively salad took a couple of minutes, if that. You don't need a recipe: the ingredients list does the job for you. Stir in as much of the elderflower dressing as you fancy, an equal amount of yoghurt (of whatever kind you favour), and give it a tweak of salt and pepper if you think it needs it.

SERVES 4 AS A SIDE

340g (12oz) fennel, finely grated
400g (14oz) rhubarb, finely chopped
200g (7oz) radishes, finely grated
small handful of dill, finely chopped
a little smoked paprika
elderflower dressing (opposite)
yoghurt

3 A tweak of salt makes it an extraordinary slap to the taste buds that really needs to be experienced, though without is probably more pleasurable.

Elderflower dressing

The pleasure of someone telling you that they've enjoyed a recipe of yours never wears off; when that someone happens to be Nigel Slater and by the way can he include it in his *Observer* column, it becomes laminated in your armoury against the days when the ideas won't come, when the words run too thick, when mediocrity pours from your fingers. It reminds you that other days are sunnier, and that they will come again.

This dressing was in my book *A Year at Otter Farm*, and it's so good I'm not about to tweak it just for the sake of it. This is its best self.

I use this on asparagus, peas, early salads and midsummer strawberries, and at this time of year when I want to call spring on a little quicker. The elderflower and rhubarb coleslaw hold hands like old friends.

2 tbsp elderflower cordial
1 tbsp white wine vinegar
1 tbsp olive oil
sea salt and freshly ground black pepper

Whisk together the cordial and vinegar, then whisk in the oil until it emulsifies. Season to taste.

Numerous willies, coppicing, Dick Whittington and hazelnut butter

I should trust the forecast. The sheets that are currently turning clockwise in the drier should be pegged to the line that hangs between the fence and the greenhouse. Today's warm wind feels two months early and is perfect for ruffling bed linen; instead, it is invisibly up to something wonderful.

In the top corner of the garden, the hazel – recently the subject of my wife's enthusiastic chopping for pea and bean poles – is hanging its lamb's tail catkins; the plant waving its many willies at anyone who cares to look. Those pale, male tassels may contain as many as three hundred flowers. The scales you can see cover four pairs of stamens: when the time is right, the scales lift, the stamens split and pollen is released.

Hazels carry female flowers separately and with much less fuss and palaver. Look up the branch a little and you might see small female buds, with their flourish of crimson. A bud might contain up to four flowers, each of which has four tiny, pink-red stigmas ready to receive pollen.[1]

When the pollen is released, you have to hope that the female flowers have pushed their stigmas into the light and – equally importantly – that there is a light breeze to carry the pollen to them. Every time pollen reaches a flower, you get one nut; so for each female bud, a cluster of perhaps four nuts.

Despite carrying male and female flowers, a hazel is self-sterile; it needs a partner. Luckily the old hedge behind the greenhouse is jammed with a few interesting species, including hazel. So if there's a breeze of just the right intensity and direction – a breeze like today's – its flowers are pollinated.

Ordinarily, a hazel might produce stamens, stigmas and nuts for 80 years; my wife's sweeps of the blade – a form of coppicing – invigorate the plant and extend that lifespan to a few hundred years. With luck, a good few generations to come will get to see what I'm seeing today on this very plant, and enjoy hazelnuts in the autumn.

---

1 This business of carrying male and female flowers separately on the same tree (rather than both within the same flower, or on separate plants) makes the plant monoecious, which – very pleasingly – is Greek for 'one household'.

Hazelnut butter

All this hazel procreation reminds me to use some of last year's harvest. As much as I love sitting by the fire, cracking them open to eat as they are, if I've a contemplative moment, I might shell a serious number for exactly this kind of thing.

Nut butters couldn't be simpler; it's all about getting the nuts to release their oils. It works equally well with almonds, walnuts and so on. It had to be crunchy peanut butter as a kid – smooth was all wrong – but now I want homemade nut butter to be granular – not quite smooth, and not quite not. I don't add sugar, unless I make a sort of Nutella by adding cocoa, when its bitterness enjoys the harmony of the sugar. Today, I split the butter into two jars, and to one added 1½ teaspoons of sugar and 1 tablespoon of cocoa: a spoon, rather than a knife, is needed with that one.

MAKES 500G (1LB 2OZ)

500g (1lb 2oz) raw hazelnuts
¾ tsp sea salt
sugar (optional)
cocoa (optional)

Preheat the oven to 170°C/150°C fan/340°F.

Spread the hazelnuts across a roasting tray in a single layer. Place in the oven for 10–12 minutes – you want the skins to colour nicely and them to smell very distantly of the first bonfire of the year. Remove from the oven and allow to cool slightly, then tip into a tea towel, bring the corners together Dick Whittington-style, and rub vigorously to encourage the dark skins to fall from the nuts. You want most off, but imperfection is fine – it adds a little smokiness.

Lift the hazelnuts into a food processor, leaving the flakes of skin behind. Add the salt. Start with the blender on low – the tone of the blade through the nuts will turn from cartoon applause to next-door neighbour's cement mixer in a few seconds. Turn it up to high and allow it to whirl, stopping and scraping down with a spatula from time to time, for 5–8 minutes, depending on the power of your processor. Soon, you'll notice the hazelnuts start to run with their own oil. Stop when it's the consistency you prefer – I like mine just a little granular – and stir in sugar and/or cocoa if you fancy.

This will keep for at least a few weeks in the fridge – not that it will last that long.

Excellent cookies, Buzzcocks, Blue Ribands and The Big Match

Dad didn't have a clue about biscuits. Once in a blue moon there would be Penguins – a source of genuine joy because it meant no Blue Ribands, his favourite. A Blue Riband has nothing to recommend it. A Jenga of wafer encased in cheap, pallid chocolate. Chocolate shouldn't sweat. Occasionally, if I was ravenous, I might convince myself that this time it would bring a sliver of satisfaction – if only from being less hungry – but no. It gave me one of the few maxims by which I live: never eat a biscuit that floats.

To make matters worse, my sister not only got to live with Mum, she got to live nearer town, nearer school, and got all the good biscuits. At Mum's, there were Trios and Breakaways;[1] their house was no stranger to a pack of Uniteds.

Everyone had better biscuits than me and Dad.

My friend Paul was in the same year at primary school. He liked space craft and knew what the letters that followed a car's name meant: he was very proud that the GL of his family's car stood for Grand Luxe. They had proper biscuits. I went round one Sunday afternoon to watch The Big Match. His mum brought us squash and a tray of Chocolate Digestives, Wagon Wheels, Viscounts and Mint Clubs. It felt like my birthday and Christmas together. The following Sunday, the same.

Paul's family were different from everyone I knew in one respect: they were Jehovah's Witnesses. I didn't know what this meant, other than it was to do with religion, and Paul told me it included not having an operation if you needed one, which sounded a bit extreme, but still: I didn't need an operation, I needed biscuits.

'Dad, I want to be a Jehovah's Witness.'

'No, son.'

'Dad, you don't understand…'

---

1 The Breakaway was made in the same Glasgow factory as the Blue Riband; you can bet your backside pilfering only happened in one part of that factory.

'Why do you want to be a Jehovah's Witness?'

'I've just been to Paul's and we had a plate of loads of different biscuits, and they do that every Sunday. I thought I could be a Jehovah's Witness and go and live with them.'

'It's a shame, as I was thinking of getting Penguins in the big shop next weekend.'

'Penguins?'

'Penguins.'

'Well, I guess there's no rush to be a Jehovah's Witness…'

As I got older, the gap between our biscuits and others' was demonstrated with every new friendship. Dave moved to our school and, like me, loved his punk and new wave. He lived in one of the new houses at the bottom of the hill. I went there after school to listen to the UK Subs (his) and Buzzcocks (mine). His mum produced a plate of Digestives that she'd iced: I could imagine no greater sophistication. The icing dissolving on the roof of my mouth combined with the crunch was better than anything I'd ever eaten.[2] It was a long walk home that afternoon.

A few years later, visits to my friend Futch's[3] house were enriched with spectacular biscuitry. His mum kept an outstanding biscuit barrel; a biscuit barrel by which all others were measured. She was an early adopter of the Hobnob – plain, milk and dark chocolate half coaters – and the chocolate chip cookie.

Then came the arrival of what we thought of as The Glamour Biscuits. Just when we were starting to get used to the idea of chocolate chip cookies – small, excellent circles studded with nuggets of chocolate and nut – their bodybuilding brethren barged on to the shelves. Rather than maybe 20 two-inch cookies to a packet, you got eight or so plump, rugged biscuits, each held – in a mark of respect and reverence – separate to its neighbour in a compartmentalised tray. These were biscuits substantial and wide enough to have terrain, to have contours. I'd run my finger over their troughs and ridges, breaking one in half to observe how the chocolate peaks that broke the surface were, like the fillings they cause, even larger beneath.

2 Apart from the pineapple fritters from the Chinese in town.
3 When we met, he was a futurist.

Of course, we had none of these at home. As if compelled to keep himself, and therefore me, eternally a step or two down the biscuit evolutionary ladder, the old man occasionally moved up to an own-brand chocolate chip cookie. The first thing I bought when I left home was a packet of dark chocolate Hobnobs and I ate every single last bastard one of them myself.

Hazelnut and chocolate cookies

There are still a great many things I will do for the promise of a good biscuit. These use my nut butter recipe (page 51), but shop-bought peanut butter will also work. As with all Glamour Biscuits, these cookies don't snap: a small with-coffee pleasure is to see how far it will bend.

MAKES 12

75g (2½oz) oats
200g (7oz) hazelnut butter
110g (3¾oz) soft light brown sugar
½ tsp bicarbonate of soda (baking soda)
pinch of fine sea salt
2 eggs, lightly beaten
60g (2¼oz) dark (bittersweet) chocolate, chopped
small handful of hazelnuts, crushed (optional)

Preheat the oven to 180°C/160°C fan/350°F and line a couple of baking sheets with baking parchment.

Blitz the oats into a flour in a food processor, then add to a bowl with the hazelnut butter, sugar, bicarbonate of soda and salt and mix until well combined. Stir in the beaten egg, just enough to incorporate, then fold in the chocolate.

Spoon 12 dollops of dough on to the baking sheets, allowing about 5cm (2in) between each. Sprinkle with crushed hazelnuts if you fancy. Bake for 10 minutes only: they may look a little shy of being done, but this gives the pleasure of a firm outer and slightly doughy centre.

Take them out of the oven and cool for 10 minutes on the baking sheet, then transfer carefully to a wire rack. Allow to cool completely, if you can.

Blackbirds, Gazza, Boulangère and 8217 Lookout Mountain

Blackbird singing in the dead of night, take this busy brain and make it still.

4.54 a.m. Third day in a row.

Is the blackbird calling me awake, or am I just waking up and there he is?

Years ago, I asked a friend who knows much about birds how she could distinguish between them all; how could their flight or song instantly identify them. You'd recognise Maradona or Gascoigne on the pitch without seeing their face – she told me – it's as easy with birds if you get to know them.

Downloading the Merlin app to my phone has been revelatory: at first, being able to confirm that the bird you are listening to is a this-in-particular brings its own thrill, but quickly it builds a small bank of knowledge – robins, chiffchaffs, thrushes and more – that bring the characters of that background chatter into the forefront of my world. It's like hearing muffled voices as you approach a pub become recognisable when you step through the door.

Of course, in all this avian chatter I don't know what anyone's *saying*, but in the scheme of pub conversation I know it's Bob talking over the general hubbub or Charlotte who has just joined the conversation.

Opening the door has made me even more inquisitive.

I discover that even ahead of the classic dawn chorus that arrives later this month it's often blackbirds that wake to sing while other birds snooze on, and often them singing longest into dusk. Earliest of all at this time of year – and often in the dark, black night – the young males sing to establish the territory they hope will be theirs for the rest of their days;[1] it is one of these that breaks my night.

My 4.54 a.m. blackbird is likely singing to the world: 'I have a partner and this is where we live'; a feathered Graham Nash singing 'Our House'.[2] He is very welcome.

1 Typically around 1,000 of them.
2 Written about the house he shared with Joni at 8217 Lookout Mountain, Laurel Canyon.

While the male sings his imagined territory into reality, the female builds the nest and incubates the eggs. The chicks – usually between three and six of them – hatch a fortnight later, grow quickly on a largely worm diet, can leave the nest after another fortnight, and take themselves off to an independent life a month later.[3]

It makes me deeply content that enriching our soil with leaf litter and compost is hugely multiplying the earthworm population; more earthworms means more blackbirds, and more blackbirds means if I am to be awake in the dark nights of early March, I'll have musical company. By mid-morning, blackbirds are largely quiet; it's robins that are making most of the noise in the garden. By mid-afternoon at this time of year the older male blackbirds – territories established long ago – sing together in what's become known as blackbird hour. What starts like a stream flowing through a flute – seemingly for the pleasure of the singing – turns slowly to a more energetic, competitive chirruping in the noisy defence of boundaries. Right now, as late winter turns towards spring, is the best time to hear this, before others – thrush and chiffchaff among them – take over; blackbirds being too busy collecting food for their chicks to join the singsong. They'll be back. In their own time, and often just after it's rained, blackbirds find their voice again to sing the summer in. I hope I'm awake to hear them.

Potato and celeriac boulangère

As with a creamy dauphinoise, potato boulangère works beautifully with backing vocals from the faintly bitter earthiness of celeriac. The sagey, miso onions here are a nod to the savoury layer found in that other marvel of potato sides that work perfectly as mains, Jansson's temptation. The final dusting of smoked paprika adds a fine punch and a dash of smokiness to go with the charred tips; I sometimes sprinkle it on when serving rather than mid-cook so that its flavours are brighter.

You can layer this in the horizontal as many do, but inspired by Joe Woodhouse's boulangère in *Your Daily Veg*, I stack them up so they look like a cross between hasselback potatoes and a tian, giving you the perfect ratio of soft and giving to crisp crunch.

All the slicing here should be as thin as you can manage.

---

3 Two more broods may be raised before the summer holidays arrive and an end to all that tiring business.

SERVES 4 AS A MAIN, 6 AS A SIDE

3 tbsp olive oil
4 onions, thinly sliced
6 garlic cloves, finely chopped
12 sage leaves, thinly sliced
2 tbsp red miso
800g (1lb 12oz) potatoes, peeled and thinly sliced
500g (1lb 2oz) celeriac (celery root), peeled, quartered and thinly sliced
350ml (12fl oz) vegetable stock
70g (2½oz) butter
2 tsp smoked paprika
sea salt and freshly ground black pepper

Preheat the oven to 180°C/160°C fan/350°F.

Heat the oil in a large pan over a medium heat and cook the onions, stirring occasionally, for 15 minutes or so, until seriously soft. Stir in the garlic, sage and miso and season with salt and pepper. Cook for 5 minutes, stirring often.

Remove from the heat and allow to cool a little.

Mix the potatoes and celeriac into the onions – I use my hands to fully incorporate everything – and season well with salt and pepper.

In a 25 x 18cm (10 x 7in) baking dish, pack the potato/celeriac mix upright like mismatched coins. Carefully pour in the stock before seasoning again.

Place in the middle of the oven and cook for 30 minutes, then dot with the butter, dust with the smoked paprika and cook for another 25 minutes or so. If a little excellent charring here and there starts to go too far, cover with foil.

Serve with greenery – a Savoy cabbage dressed in a good, sharp dressing or some purple sprouting broccoli work perfectly.

Wild garlic, two big toenails, green goddess and panch phoron

It's not every day you lose both big toenails. Nine years, two months and ten days ago, I did just that.

Walking from my East Devon hometown towards West Dorset, eyes to the sun, sea to the right, is as good a day as there is. The second half is as undulating as it is beautiful, and by 'undulating' I mean it's an absolute bastard.

Walking steeply downhill can be as tiring as walking up: insteps stretching away from you, knees locking, toes jamming into the front of your boots with all your weight behind them.

As sunset turned to all-but-darkness, my feet felt for a path down the dimpsy final decline into Branscombe, me desperate for a bath and beer, and for the welcome car headlights I saw turning into the car park below.

It wasn't until two days later that both toenails turned purple, and that I fully appreciated the madness of unworn-in boots, undeployed nail scissors and steep declines jamming those nails back into their toes. A fortnight later, painlessly, those toenails let go of their owner.

It is that last dark decline that is today's bright incline, retracing my steps towards a glorious view and a patch of woodland just as the slope crests. As winter thinks about spring, much of this wood fills with wild garlic.

A wide swathe follows the coast path for a few hundred yards of the highest ground, thickly carpeting an opening to greet climbing legs. Much is reassuringly far from the path to assume a dog might be disinterested in reaching it.

Wild garlic is – after blackberries and elderflower – the most familiar and easiest of wild harvests. There's no mistaking it: the squeak of the blade through taut cellulose brings fresh, bright garlic to the nostrils. Lookalikes such as Lily of the Valley and bluebells – that you most certainly do not want to eat – carry none of that potent fragrance. If you have a nose, you can't go wrong.

More competitive foragers may have been here a fortnight ago, but their reward for the earliest wild garlic is smaller, grassier and without the intensity that is almost – but crucially not quite – too much. Now, the leaves have reached 15–20cm (6–8in) long: they're bright and tight, and to my mind at their very best.

On and off, for twenty years, my wife and I – and occasionally our daughter – have trudged this path to stretch our legs, walk off lunch or a pint, and to pick wild garlic. Those two decades of familiarity and connection make here seem part of my virtual garden, as much 'mine' as the garden itself.

Of course – and happily – it isn't mine, but today, with a sharp easterly cutting my ankles off at the knees, there are few people on the coast path. An older couple ask what I'm picking, and – seeing my camera – do I publish my photography: by peculiar coincidence, they know someone with the same surname. There's a curious friendliness about being on a coast path that differs from one inland, and I've no idea why.[1]

I remind myself – as I always do – that the clearing above the wild garlic, which opens out beautifully looking across the bay to Lyme one way and Teignmouth the other, would be the perfect place for a sunny mid-spring picnic. Maybe this year I'll finally remember to pack a rucksack filled with small jars of this and wrapped slices of that, with a blanket that feels special enough to eat from but not enough to be precious about.

When I pick elderflower, I'm entirely full of anticipation about everything I'm going to make with it; with wild garlic it's a much gentler pleasure – and a great deal of it is in marking what is almost upon us: spring.

I have little time for the familiar pesto; twice a year, ideally on squeaky green beans and potatoes rather than pasta, is plenty for me. Wild garlic pesto may be my least favourite way with wild garlic; its delightful nasally character seems to turn funky and harsh. Instead, I turn to a similar yet far superior sauce – my take on green goddess dressing.

I often leave wild garlic in a full sink to soak off any detritus for half a day. Later in the afternoon, I sift through the leaves: there's often – as there is today – some ivy and a few other unidentifiables that are worth extricating.

1 That's not quite true. Many years ago, I almost fell into academia, having gone from deeply idle (though excellent at pool and drinking) to accidentally excelling at university. I was particularly interested in landscape and perception. A very interesting man – Jay Appleton – came up with prospect and refuge theory; essentially, that we are drawn to, and feel at home in, environments where we have both prospect (the ability to observe opportunities or foresee dangers) and refuge (the ability to hide or remain concealed from danger). He proposed that everything from architecture, room design and even our appreciation of art might be better understood with this theory in mind.

Green goddess dressing

So wet and grey has winter been, that my ongoing mood is for roasted vegetables of one kind or another; it might be the warmth of the oven as much as the food that I'm craving.

Almost always, I want a sauce or dressing to go with them. Sometimes it's tahini-based for the nuttiness of the sesame; often, something creamier like this wild garlic green goddess dressing. A few spoonfuls of this with new potatoes, roasted meat of whatever kind, a handful of griddled asparagus, or the carrots overleaf is so good. I tend to freeze half to enjoy once the wild garlic season has passed.

MAKES ABOUT 1 LITRE (1¾ PINTS)

a salad spinner generously filled with wild garlic
25g (1oz) mint, leaves only
200g (7oz) mayonnaise
200g (7oz) plain yoghurt, of whatever kind you favour
3 tbsp extra virgin olive oil
3 tbsp capers
½ tbsp sea salt
juice of 1 lemon
freshly ground black pepper

Whizz everything in a blender, set to high, until incorporated. Taste the dressing and season with freshly ground black pepper and more salt as needed.

Panch phoron roast carrots with green goddess dressing

I make a different variation of this recipe every time: often like this as a side for four, occasionally as a main by doubling or trebling the volume with some or all of potatoes, quartered fennel, shallots, Jerusalem artichokes and beetroot.

The Bengali/Bangladeshi spice blend panch phoron is one of my favourites, bringing instant brilliance when serving soup, finishing lentils or sprinkled over eggs. Panch translates as five and phoron as spice, so strictly speaking this should be chhah (six) phoron as I've added coriander; coriander – being more perfume than flavour – works so well with the dressing's punch. The quantities below will make more than you need.

SERVES 4 AS A SIDE

700g (1½lb) small carrots
50ml (2fl oz) extra virgin olive oil
2 tsp panch phoron (see below)
1 tsp sea salt
a few good pinches of paprika
good grinding of black pepper
green goddess dressing (page 64)
50g (2oz) almonds, lightly toasted in a dry pan and crushed
1 tsp sesame seeds, lightly toasted in a dry pan

FOR THE PANCH PHORON (SIMPLY COMBINE IN A JAR)

1 tbsp cumin seeds
1 tbsp fennel seeds
1 tbsp nigella seeds
1 tbsp fenugreek seeds
1 tbsp mustard seeds
1 tbsp coriander seeds

Preheat the oven to 190°C/170°C fan/375°F. Place the carrots in a bowl with everything but the almonds, sesame seeds and dressing and toss to coat. Tip on to a roasting tray and roast for 20–25 minutes until tender and taking on a little colour here and there.

Spoon the carrots on to a serving dish. Spatter with a few spoonfuls of dressing (or more, to your taste), sprinkle with almonds and sesame seeds and serve immediately.

Alexanders, ice cream, Saturday punks and the *Spirit of Eden*

Call me old-fashioned, but I like to end the day as unpoisoned as I started it. So I take foraging very seriously. The main way I go about this is by not foraging very often.[1] Occasionally my greedy stomach wins, even when I read that the treasure for which I am about to go in search can be mistaken for something that might do me a mischief.

At this time of year, Alexanders is everywhere in my patch of South West England. You'll find it in coastal areas,[2] growing in great swathes along verges, cliffs, footpaths and on the edge of woods.

Everywhere the dog and I walk, a flush of its lime green leaves and lemon yellow flowers greets us.

Known back in the day as the parsley of Alexandria, and much more part of our diet than it is now, Alexanders is a real foragers' favourite. Every foraging bible tells you to beware of the other plants with which you might confuse Alexanders, for it is a mistake you are unlikely to repeat.

I am positive that what carpets the top of the cliffs is Alexanders, but still I check the books to be sure that the scent of the crushed stems – a peculiarly spicy fragrance – is as it should be, and that the leaves are indeed gently notched rather than the heavily incised leaves of the entirely less friendly hemlock.

I text my old pal Tim who knows everything on such matters, and he reassures me that – given my photo and description – I am more likely to die crossing the road from the car to the cliff than from eating it. I am grateful to him, but feel he also has some duty here, as it was he who introduced me to Alexanders in the first place.

---

1 At school there was little more damning than being called a Saturday punk, implying you were square all week and your hair went vertical on a Friday night for two days. I am most definitely a Saturday forager, but an enthusiastic one nonetheless.
2 Its likely origin is the Canary Islands, so the milder the better.

There are several rules I follow when foraging, chief among them is to take the dog. If you don't have a dog, borrow one. In the mind of the casual observer, a dog turns a peeping Tom into a nature lover, a knife-wielding maniac into a considerate wild harvester, from someone to be avoided to someone to pass the time of day with.

A great deal of the plant is not only edible, it's delicious (a distinction not made by every foraging book for every wild food). If I come back in a few weeks the flowers will be good; later still I can pick seeds to grind like pepper.

Today, I've brought a sharp knife wrapped in a tea towel (it's these small details that prevent arrest). I'm interested in the top 20cm (8in) or so; mostly leaves but with a good deal of stalky scaffolding. I leave them in a deep sinkful of water for an hour, shake them off and then set about making ice cream.

A couple of days later, my wife asked me to step into the garden. This isn't usually a good sign. Often it necessitates an apology for me leaving the new fork out in the rain, perhaps a rake left – tines up – awaiting an unsuspecting foot and a subsequent rap on the nose; occasionally it might be to watch a woodpecker taking its breakfast from the creatures living in the grass. Today, she asks me if I know what the large plant living next to the not entirely dissimilar sweet cicely is. No idea, I say. That's hemlock, she tells me, the very plant I was concerned about Alexanders not being.

I pull it up, with the aid of that fork I'd left out in the rain.

It is peculiarly sobering to be in the company of something as everyday, and as seemingly benign, as a plant that would see the end of my life if I ate so much as half a dozen leaves of it. I'd have an hour or two to listen to my favourite album,[3] eat as many spoonfuls of dauphinoise and trifle, and drink as many mojitos, as possible, before the small matter of muscular paralysis, respiratory failure and death would draw a strong line under what until that point had been looking like an excellent end to the day.

What I'm struck by is just how very different the leaves of hemlock look from Alexanders', and how once you have made a friend of one, it is only superficially mistakable for the other.

---

3 Talk Talk's *Spirit of Eden*.

Both are of the Apiaceae family – aka the umbellifers – to which celery, carrot and parsley also belong. The leaves of Alexanders look much more like large fleshy parsley leaves, and hemlock's much more like carrots'.

So while I was out there in the wild, double and triple checking in an attempt to go to bed unpoisoned, the danger was only a few yards from my kitchen, quietly growing, partly hidden by the emerging deliciousness of other plants, its malign form blind to me by virtue of it being in a place I assumed was full of only the harmless and delicious.

Alexanders ice cream

I met Tim Maddams back in the early days of River Cottage – he was chef at the RC Axminster Stores and was involved in many of the events at RCHQ. He was quite the bolshy bastard at the time, which – I confess – I find fascinating in people. He also kept giving the game away that he was one of the very good guys, that his sensitive side was rather more pronounced than he might have liked to let on.

Quite a few years later, when life was not at its greatest, he showed up. As the old saying goes, when people show you who they are, believe them, and he did that in all the simple, positive ways I had no right to expect. And will never forget.

He put on a fabulous feast night for us at the old place, and dessert included Alexanders ice cream. Despite the farm being home to perhaps the greatest diversity of edible plants in the country, this one was a flavour I'd never tried.

Like a mulberry, it is hard to navigate accurately to its uniqueness via others, but the right ballpark is somewhere between rhubarb, parsley, cucumber and a distant unnameable spice. It's really entirely unique and I love it.

This is Tim's recipe – dictated in a series of WhatsApp voice notes in that mix of precision and feel you get from a chef – with exact proportions adjusted based on tasting the warm ice cream, as Tim suggested, and with a little tweak of vanilla extract to soften the grassiness, my own idea.

Thank you, Tim.

MAKES 1 LITRE (1¾ PINTS)

500ml (18fl oz) double (heavy) cream
500ml (18fl oz) whole milk
140g (4½oz) brown sugar
5 egg yolks
½ tsp vanilla extract
12 or so 20cm (8in) long stems of Alexanders

In a large pan, stir together half the cream, half the milk and all of the sugar over a medium heat until the sugar has dissolved.

Whisk the yolks together, then pour them in, stirring constantly. Bring to a simmer and whisk as it thickens into a smooth custard. Stir in the vanilla extract. Take off the heat.

Place the Alexanders in a blender, along with two ladlefuls of the warm custard and blend on high until smooth. Add the remaining custard and blend to fully combine. Pour into a cold dish, stirring in the rest of the cold milk and cream to help cool it quickly.

Once at room temperature, churn in an ice-cream maker and freeze.

Bay flowers, Gene Wilder, a biblical wait and an Airfix aeroplane

Three days after the old man went toes up, I took a stiff cardboard box to the house where I'd spent my first 18 years and he his last 34. It was like he'd gone to the shops. If I'd put the kettle on, he'd be back before it boiled.

I sat in his chair for a minute, scrunched a piece of paper from his pad and threw it at the bin at the far end of the sofa; as a kid, he never seemed to miss – the crushed fag packet hitting the inside with a clang.

Before filling the box with a few old pictures, an Airfix plane we'd done together when I was a kid and other oddments, I stood in my old bedroom for the last time. On the door frame, wrinkled gloss that looked to six-year-old me like Jesus' face, still there. On the landing, a window that looked over the back garden; still attached to the curtain, a quarter of a century after it had been pinned there, a badge that had been hand-coloured with two letters – A and R – by primary school me.

AR stood for Advanced Reader. I may be the world's slowest, most easily distractible reader, but for a few short days when the sun was shining and the teacher was looking, I chewed through *Charlie and the Chocolate Factory* quicker than I could see off a Cadbury's Curly Wurly.[1] I was awarded a plain badge to colour with the two letters that broadcast my new status. I saw the film soon after and fell even deeper under the story's spell. If you haven't seen it (or, worse, have only seen later versions) all you need to see is Wonka's entrance to know what's ahead.[2]

1 For reasons unclear, some confectionery must have the maker's name spoken or written as part of it, while others most definitely not. Cadbury's Curly Wurly, Terry's Chocolate Orange and Nestlé Milky Bar are classics of the former; the Fudge, Lion Bar and Matchmakers examples of the latter.
2 When offered the role, Gene Wilder had one stipulation to accepting for director Mel Stuart:

Wilder: When I make my first entrance, I'd like to come out of the door carrying a cane and then walk toward the crowd with a limp. After the crowd sees Willy Wonka is a cripple, they all whisper to themselves and then become deathly quiet. As I walk toward them, my cane sinks into one of the cobblestones I'm walking on and stands straight up, by itself; but I keep on walking, until I realise that I no longer have my cane. I start to fall forward, and just before I hit the ground, I do a beautiful forward somersault and bounce back up, to great applause.

Stuart: What do you want to do that for?

Wilder: From that time on, no one will know if I'm lying or telling the truth.

I think it is Wilder's Wonka that left me with the childhood urge to play with ingredients. That first half term I was left alone at home, I was sure I'd found my fortune – a drink called cofftea that needs neither explanation nor repetition. Soon after, at a friend's house, it seemed a good idea to pour a centimetre from every bottle of spirits into a glass in the search for the until-then undiscovered finest drink in the universe. That day didn't end well.

A few days ago, a conversation with an excellent friend about bay flowers had me wondering whether an old favourite of a bay recipe might work with the flowers rather than the leaves. I have no idea whether any of the leaves' spicy, vanilla, clovey cola flavour is carried by the flowers, but the sliver of half-term me that still inhabits this larger version fancied trying it.

This rare sunny morning, fresh from a walk to the beach and back, I caught the flowers' honeyed scent, livened, I'm sure, by the bright sun hitting them. It smelled like relief.

'Are you sure they are edible?' my wife asked.

'No idea,' I replied. That's for googling later.[3]

I'd rather not obstruct the lightbulb in my brain: I might be making poison, it might be bang average, or it might be the golden ticket. Let's hope that, like Violet Beauregarde, I'm not turned into the equivalent of a giant blueberry after chewing Wonka's experimental gum.

I'll let you know.[4] And if you have – or know of – a bay in flower nearby, why not join me: what's to lose other than a jarful of gin and quarter of an hour with your nose in a bay tree.

Wonka's allorino

Fill a jar 40 per cent full of bay flowers and top with gin. Leave until it tastes nice. I have no idea how long this might be but I will taste in weekly intervals.

Sugar may need to be added. Let's see.

---

3 I can find nothing to suggest bay flowers are in any way harmful.
4 3rd June me tells you it's very good.

Blackberry allorino

When chatting with that old friend, she asked if I'd ever tried blackberry and bay together as it was extraordinary. I couldn't remember having done, and so I set about making a berry version of the allorino recipe in my book *Herb*.

I had some berries from last summer's harvest in the freezer, but if you haven't and prefer to dodge the overseas berries in the shops at this time of year, treble the number of bay leaves and leave out the fruit for a more traditional version.

Dried bay leaves tend to be stronger (so consider adding a third less); I prefer the more cola flavour of fresh.

Of the many Biblical tales that were cast at an impervious young me by a squadron of kindly Sunday school nuns, the story of Jesus being tempted by the devil in the Judaean Desert is one of the few that fascinated. His ordeal of restraint lasted 40 days and 40 nights, and here I recreate this period of sufferance not in the search for spiritual nourishment but divine intoxication. The wait is worth it.

The Italian for bay leaf is *foglia d'alloro*, hence this liqueur's name. In the glass, without the blackberries, it may resemble dentist swill but there the similarity ends: this works perfectly as a room-temperature comforter in front of the fire, an icy digestivo at either bookend of a good meal, or an on-the-rocks summer sizzler with Prosecco.

6 bay leaves
100g (3½oz) caster (superfine) sugar
350ml (12fl oz) vodka
150g (5oz) blackberries

Wash the bay leaves and tear them a little to accelerate the infusion process. Add the sugar and half the vodka to a large jar and shake to encourage the sugar to start to dissolve. Add the remaining ingredients. Invert every day you remember, to keep the sugar dissolving. Leave to infuse for 40 days.

Asparagus, sweet cicely, a Venn diagram and the colour of spring

It won't stop raining. It won't stop raining long enough for a lame sun to brighten the 56 pages of *Don't Look Now* I'm trying to read. It won't stop raining long enough to half-fill a barrow of weeds without the soil turning to sludge. And it won't stop raining long enough for the sun to encourage the seedlings towards it.

It is, at least, elastic band season. Between now and the end of May I'll acquire all the rubber bands I need for the year. Small packets of red lentils and black, that open pack of coffee beans, and the half-finished bag of penne, all safely secured thanks to my enthusiasm for asparagus.

Heartbreakingly, I don't grow what is perhaps my favourite vegetable, as it takes so much room for a few short weeks of productivity – which would be fine if it didn't need to be entirely without even friendly neighbours for the entire year. Asparagus doesn't suit polyculture. So I buy it, and with it all the elastic bands I need.

I may not have home-grown asparagus, but I do have sweet cicely. And it's beautiful.

I owe its now-longtime acquaintance to my father-in-law. Getting on for twenty years ago, when I mentioned I liked the sound of it, his face lit up that I might relieve him of numerous self-seeded plants that were more nuisance than ornament to him. As a result, I happily occupy the centre of an affectionate Venn diagram with sweet cicely on one side and he on the other.

There are a few herbs that make you wonder how you got by before you knew them, and sweet cicely is one.[1] Its flavour and fragrance is a sweet coming together of fennel, liquorice and star anise, all of which contain its essential oil, anethole.

It is so good with shellfish, stone fruit, rhubarb and most certainly asparagus and eggs. It has another gift, as botanist John Parkinson wrote in the 17th-century: 'It gives a better taste to any other herb put with it.' It is a catalyser, one whose qualities fade behind others

---

1 If you don't have sweet cicely in your life, you really ought to do something about that.

it uplifts: chop it with parsley and it'll appear more parsleyish without sweet cicely seeming present. This ability to enhance other herbs' flavour – as well as being a delight on its own – makes it a favourite in France, Scandinavia and northern Germany in particular. As John P alludes, it was once used commonly here in the UK, where the implied sweetness of its gentle aniseed lessens the need for adding sugar to rhubarb and other sharp fruits.

Every part is edible. Its incised, fern-like leaves emerge first, followed quickly by small white flowers, creating a fair impersonation of cow parsley. I love how sweet cicely displays its life cycle – leaf to flower to seed – within a few short weeks. By the time spring has settled in, it might reach a metre tall, catching any whiff of breeze that might be passing, bees drawn to those frothy white flowers.

The seeds – little, ridged, liquorice comfits – are most intensely flavoured and they'll get to 3cm (1in) or so long. Eat them while they're green; the texture and flavour declines as they turn brown. Any that fall on to fertile ground will – as my father-in-law found – readily germinate: eating them is the surest way to avoid self-seeding. If you save seeds to start off in modules, sow before winter as they need a period of cold to germinate. I take the easy road and usually let a few seeds fall where they like, relocating any seedlings that result: they're free plants and – equally importantly – doing so reminds me of my father-in-law, of whom I am very fond.

Sweet cicely doesn't mind the cold,[2] so in mild locations you might be able to harvest it through winter, but here in the UK it usually retreats against the chill. I'm particularly grateful, if I'm honest: the fact that it comes back at the first sign of lengthening days helps me believe spring proper will soon arrive.

Today, somewhat worn down by the overcast (at best) and torrential (more usual) conditions, I felt the need for sweet cicely and asparagus' implied springtime. I put on Talk Talk's *The Colour of Spring*, cook and pretend.

---

2 Should you find yourself wandering the mountain pastures from the Pyrenees to the Caucasus, you will almost certainly come across sweet cicely growing wild; so too, in the hills of Wales, northern England and Scotland. And, more intentionally, in my rainy corner of Devon.

Asparagus and spring onion frittata

This is just about thick enough to deserve the name frittata, but I wouldn't argue if you called it an omelette. The work of perhaps 10 minutes from thought to fork, it partners three of my favourite spring ingredients to glorious effect. If you haven't any sweet cicely, this works very well with tarragon instead.

SERVES 2

10 spring onions (scallions)
7–8 asparagus spears, tough ends snapped off and discarded
2 tbsp olive oil
1 fat garlic clove (or 2 slim), finely chopped
6 eggs, lightly whisked
small handful of sweet cicely (or tarragon), roughly chopped
sea salt and freshly ground black pepper

Halve (or quarter, if large) the spring onions lengthways. Use a peeler to shave thin slices from the asparagus – start just below the tip, towards the base, taking slices alternately from opposite sides – leaving a thin slice attached to the tip.

Warm the oil in a frying pan of around 25cm (10in) across. Add the spring onions and cook for 4 minutes, stirring occasionally. Add the asparagus and cook for a further 4 minutes, then add the garlic and cook, stirring a few times, for 2 minutes.

Pour in the eggs and allow to cook undisturbed for a couple of minutes. Sprinkle with sweet cicely, a good pinch of salt and some pepper.

Take the pan off the heat and place a plate over it. Using oven gloves, flip the pan over, turning the frittata on to the plate. Slide the frittata, cooked side up, back into the pan – a little untidiness here is not unusual – and cook for another few minutes.

If you feel the need for greenery, a couple of quartered, dressed little gems are very good here, but I'm most likely to eat this from the pan, sprinkled with too much salt, picking at it with a fork.

Sauce gribiche, a random wind, Johnny Marr and moonlanding wallpaper

You can tell a lot about a tin can from the noise it makes as it tracks down the road at 2.27 a.m.

It's no longer a cylinder – I'm sure of it: it has dents, perhaps squished towards two dimensions for recycling – otherwise the wind, Storm Whatever, would've picked it up by now. Instead, it stitches its rattling stop-start way slowly down the hill towards the nice man at No.1.

Do I risk being pulled brightly awake time and again by its intermittent tune, or lift myself out of bed and into the gale to retrieve it?

I nod off.

> *I am eight. I'm as happy as can be, lying to attention, sheets and blankets tucked in as tight as Mum can do them. Apart from turning my head left and right, I can't move. Cold sheets slowly warming to a perfect cocoon. I am just about ok to have the landing light off, but in winter I like the curtains open: if a UFO spins its flashing path towards Donkey Hill, I don't want to miss it. The moon is high and fat; blue and grey clouds draw slowly across it. My wallpaper repeats the same moon in cartoon miniature, astronauts stepping from their craft to its cratered landscape; it is brought to flickering life by the streetlight casting its brilliance through the tall tree by the road. The wind is up. An empty can races towards the churchyard, a metal bin lid giving unconvincing chase. Below my bedroom, an overgrown branch scratches against the front room window. Headlights gallop thick shadows across my wall and over my head. I slip back into sleep.*

The tin can steel band strikes up again, and I'm hauled from the bottom of the well, awake.

A random can, one of a gazillion made in a factory, filled in a factory, finding its random way to being opened in a kitchen in my road, placed in the top of a recycling bin, so that the weather can pick it out from the ill-closed lid. What are the chances.

I really ought to get up and sort it, as tonight will be a late one. Impossibly 41 years after I first saw him in The Smiths, I am going to see Johnny Marr with my daughter, she impossibly the same age I was when I saw him/them all those years ago. Just two years after that first time, at only 23, Marr's tin can had completed most of its holy journey – changing popular music for ever – despite whatever brilliance he followed it with. What do you do with that, aged 23?[1] Turn up, create, show that you are still a charming man in whatever form that takes, and make everyone very happy.[2]

Sod getting up and into this wind; I turn over.

The clink of glass in the dark. The milk float's stopping outside. Not long until I have to get up for school, but not quite yet. He's whistling again – who whistles at night? Maybe he's giving ghosts or burglars notice he's coming. I can hear his shoes clicking on the path that runs from the road; the path that brings good news and bad to us and Kay next door. His whistle turns echoey and muffled as the path becomes a covered alley. At the back, a pair of gates, set at an angle to each other: the left one takes you into Kay's back garden, the right one into ours. Here a small crate by the back door: I can hear him replace the empties with fresh bottles. I hope the blue tits don't peck through the foil, eager, as I am, for the cream. I need it for my Weetabix.

5.13 a.m. Awake again: a bottle clanks against the road. I'm ravenous for Weetabix, cream and brown sugar. Then I remember there's sauce gribiche in the fridge. It's a close second and just enough of an incentive. Time to get up and put that can and bottle in the bin.

---

1 I don't think it's any coincidence that The Beatles, Joy Division and The Smiths were all working-class lads with a plan no more complex than the love of making music, each touched by genius, but maybe more importantly blessed with the luck to be randomly picked up by Storm Whatever that just happened to be blowing down their road.
2 I will undoubtedly cry at some point, for the teenager who found some beautiful (and certainly sanity-saving) connection with what they created, and for the middle-aged man transported for a couple of hours into that still-present teenager so very grateful to have found something he loves doing, when he had no inkling at that age that he ever might.

Sauce gribiche

I make no secret of my love for the egg/mayo combination – you should also try my recipe for herby eggs on toast from my book *Herb* – and this incredible French classic is a beautifully elegant embellishment on this theme. It is one of my very favourite things: try it with quartered, charred little gems, poached leeks, smoked mackerel or asparagus and toast as I've chosen this morning.

To my taste, it should have enough vinegar to gently tweak your nose; ease back just a touch if you'd rather. Once again, sweet cicely and/or chervil are so very good here, but the more widely available parsley and tarragon make such a good tribute band that you won't miss them.

MAKES ENOUGH FOR 6 PORTIONS OF THE RECIPE ON THE NEXT PAGE

6 eggs
2 large egg yolks
450ml (15fl oz) extra virgin olive oil
5 tsp white wine vinegar
1 tbsp Dijon mustard
16 cornichons, roughly chopped
3 tbsp capers, chopped
small half bunch of flat-leaf parsley, finely chopped
small half bunch of tarragon, leaves only, finely chopped
sea salt and freshly ground black pepper

Bring a half-full medium pan of water to the boil and lower to a simmer. Lower the eggs in carefully with a spoon. Simmer for 7 minutes, or 30 seconds longer if the eggs are large.

Take off the heat and immediately run cold water into the pan continuously for a minute – this rapid cooling makes the eggs easier to handle and ensures no dark ring around the yolk.

Peel each egg. Cut through the equator of the white of an egg, extracting the firm yolk. Repeat for each egg. Chop the egg white somewhere between rough and fine.

In a medium bowl, mash the cooked and raw yolks together. Whisk in a little of the oil, making sure it is fully incorporated before adding a little more. Repeat in increments, adding a little more oil than the last time, until all thickly emulsified. Stir in the vinegar, mustard, cornichons, capers, chopped egg white and herbs. Add a generous pinch of salt, a heavy black peppering, and taste, seasoning more if needed.

This should stay glorious for 3 days or so in the fridge – just give it a stir to perk it up.

Asparagus and sauce gribiche on toast

In the absence of Weetabix with cream and brown sugar, this makes a perfect breakfast, brunch, lunch or even a quick pleasing supper.

The small details make all the difference here, most especially the freshness of the asparagus and the excellence of the eggs. Hold the asparagus towards the base and bend it; it should snap. If it bends more than a little, make soup with it and acquire some fresher asparagus: nothing good ever comes of entertaining something that resembles Gonzo's nose when firmness is required.

Much as I love roasted asparagus, I'm not putting the oven on especially for it,[3] and in any event, the squeakiness that comes with a quick simmering suits the sauce beautifully. I dust the whole lot with paprika, but if you fancy chilli powder (or even chaat) instead, on you go.

Bring a good-sized pan a third-full of water to the boil. Toast some bread.

Lower a handful of asparagus into the water, base first, the tips resting on the rim – this isn't critical, but if they stay there for a moment until the stems soften just enough to bend and draw the tips underwater, they will get the shorter cooking they ideally require.

I don't butter the toast – this is already richer than a Chelsea midfielder – but go ahead if you are desperate to.

Lay the asparagus on the toast, spoon over as little or much of the gribiche as you like – I like almost as much as if it were scrambled egg – and dust generously with paprika.

---

3 Unless it's the first asparagus of the season, when all anticipation must be satisfied.

Hot cars, pruning, herb flowers and a spring gratin

Can there be a better smell than a car interior on the first hot day of the year? It is – like afternoon sex in June, a long early evening bath in late October, and the freezing back/ roasting face of a bonfire in January – a pleasure multiplied by the time of the year.

Saturday – in perception and very possibly reality – was the first seriously sunny day since mid-September. It wasn't just bright; it had heat. A third of me that I hadn't known was missing came out of hibernation.

I tore into pruning, strimming, weeding and digging as if it all had to be done today. It reminded me of 20 years ago in the old farm's early days when I'd plant 50 trees between breakfast and sleep, metre cubes of tough pasture excavated to accommodate the existing roots and allow for a season or two of easy growth. On Saturday, I realised how much I missed the feeling of working in the physical zone of doing, where I don't notice scratches and cuts.

The trips to the tip, back seats down and covered in prunings from neighbours' overhanging trees and shrubs, and trugs heaving with perennial garden weeds, needed windows down. My thoughts turned to a perspiring glass of cider. I think a little of me had begun to wonder if a day was ever going to feel like this again.

After, a late afternoon stroll around my wife's allotment – the warmth dipping off quicker than it came – gave me the chance to pluck a few flowers from the clumps of wild garlic and three-cornered leek that are safe from dogs' attentions. Pinched at the top of their stem, their clusters whole, with the sun having woken their oils, these were easy, flavourful rewards I knew would transform the evening meal.

The day was from late June and the evening from October, and this gratin – with one foot in the new season and the other in the old – suited it perfectly.

Sprouting broccoli, asparagus and spring flower gratin

I make versions of this throughout the year, with chard or tenderstem, perhaps whole leeks or celery, or cauliflower or broccoli stepping in for the sprouting broccoli and asparagus. A wide, shallow dish makes the seasoned cream more of a dressing than a classic gratin sauce, and goes perfectly with the crunch. And while not essential, the flowers pop little darts of punctuation through this, and the pleasure of the simple harvest makes it feel very much of the season and of the day. Serve with quartered little gems or a green salad dressed just with olive oil and salt.

SERVES 3 AS A MAIN, OR 4 AS A SIDE

2 fat leeks, trimmed and sliced into 3cm (1in) pieces
3 tbsp olive oil
300g (10oz) sprouting broccoli
400g (14oz) asparagus, tough bases snapped off
finely grated zest of 1 lemon
20cm (8in) stem of rosemary, leaves only, finely chopped
220ml (7½fl oz) double (heavy) cream
40g (1½oz) walnuts, roughly chopped
20g (¾oz) sunflower seeds
20g (¾oz) pumpkin seeds
2 tsp fennel seeds
35g (1¼oz) Parmesan, grated
handful of rosemary, three-cornered leek and wild garlic flowers
sea salt and freshly ground black pepper

Preheat the oven to 200°C/180°C fan/400°F.

Place the leeks in a single layer on a baking dish, drizzle with olive oil, season with salt and pepper and roast for 15–20 minutes until cooked through and colouring in places.

Add the sprouting broccoli to a pan of boiling salted water, place the asparagus on top (so only the base of the spears are fully submerged) and cook for 1 minute only. Drain.

Stir the lemon zest, rosemary and a good scrunch of salt and pepper into the cream. Stir the walnuts and seeds together.

Arrange the broccoli and asparagus on top of the leeks, pour over the seasoned cream and scatter with the nut/seed mix. Season with salt and pepper and bake for a further 15–20 minutes. Scatter with the Parmesan and flowers and serve.

Elaeagnus, Hawaii, lovage and Robert Duvall

A garden is a place of ghosts. Not all of them people, and few of them dead. If I'm out there – for a minute or a day – faces are called to mind, places revisited, moments relived.

Pruning the neighbours' overhanging *Elaeagnus ebbingei* last week revealed a couple-dozen small oval fruit in the tangle of branches. They aren't much to write home about, if truth be told – to call them 'astringent' does them a kindness – but they're ok, and the many birds that take them are most welcome.

I love Elaeagnus for two more substantial reasons. All Elaeagnus species take nitrogen from the air and use it to feed themselves, making the excess available in the soil for neighbouring plants, while the leaves of deciduous varieties also share their nitrogen as they decompose, wherever the wind drops them. One way or another, Elaeagnus nourish the garden and some of the creatures who live and pass through it. In the old place, I planted a few between Asian pears, in the understory of a peach and alongside a row of pecans; great rows of *Elaeagnus umbellata* – autumn olive – bordered and defined orchards and threw their life-giving nutrients to the crops either side.

The early autumn flowers that precede the fruit are unremarkable from a distance, yet cute as hell close up; best of all, their scent is utterly transporting.[1] The invisible fragrant clouds they release are unreliable, turning up when they like, and leaving when they fancy. For reasons unknown,[2] and as with quince, you push your nose into the blossom and the perfume is mild or absent; turn to leave, and a few paces away it fills the senses. You can't chase it, it comes to you. Elaeagnus reminds me of an American friend, Trent, who worked at our old farm. I'd always wanted a friend with a surname for a first name; a major disappointment was him not using an initial either before or after his first name, but he knew more than I did about looking after a vineyard, so I made allowances. On the way in from picking grapes, he stopped in his tracks.

'Oh man, what is that?'

'That's the *Elaeagnus ebbingei*.'

'I know that smell, I'd know it anywhere. Give me a minute…'

---

1 It is as close as I know to the scent of broad bean flowers, which might be my favourite fragrance of all.
2 To me at least.

I kept quiet, allowing him to empty his head as he stared at the sky. He buried his face in the plant. No joy. We walked on a few paces and the invisible cloud found him.

Like Robert Duvall in *Apocalypse Now*, he felt for the words.

'I've got it. It smells like… Hawaii!'

Anytime since then when I smell it, prune it or plant it, I think of Trent,[3] and when I smell that scent I imagine an island I'll likely never visit, my mind knowing it a little better despite life keeping us apart.

As I uncovered each Elaeagnus fruit, I threw it down on to the softest landing pad available: the compost of a large pot of Scots lovage. Lovage is the definition of Sod's Law: such is its bitter, savoury intensity, you need only very little in the kitchen, yet it grows briskly, in its indestructible way, requiring numerous dedicated attempts on its life to keep it under control. Scots (aka Scotch) lovage is a considerably smaller, rounder-leaved – a more succulent variation – and perfect for a container by the kitchen door. Rather than make something with the Elaeagnus fruit in the pot – which would please no one – I pinched a few leaves of lovage for this superb sundowner.

Rhubarb and lovage gimlet

For the lovage syrup stir 250ml (9fl oz) boiling water into 300g (10oz) caster sugar until it dissolves. Throw in a handful of lovage leaves and allow to infuse while it cools – taste it now and again; when it is good and strong discard the leaves. A juicer will reduce rhubarb stems to a sharp, pale pink liquid in an instant, otherwise use a good cloudy apple juice. The lime juice is yours to judge: typically, I find half a juicy lime about right.

SERVES 1

25ml (1fl oz) gin
25ml (1fl oz) rhubarb juice
25ml (1fl oz) lovage syrup
lime juice, to taste

Add everything plus ice to a cocktail shaker and shake for half a minute or so, straining into a suitable glass. If you are without a shaker, use a jar and strain through a sieve.

3 Trent is now making incredible saddlery and leading horse treks through the hills of West Coast America.

Cardoons, woodlice, Caramac and *Apios americana*

A blackbird is sat on the chimney, singing its little heart out. Unbeknown to it, the pot right by its feathery arse funnels its song, magnified by the chimney's lining, to be broadcast live and loud in the kitchen three floors below where I am stirring a white sauce for tonight's supper.

After a day of actual sunshine, what seemed impossible just an hour ago: the wind turned and the rain lashes down. That blackbird isn't bothered one bit. It's been singing like this two or three times a day. Only once have I not stopped to listen: this morning, when carrying egg boxes of potatoes from the sunny windowsill where they've been chitting to their new home in the garden.

I don't believe anyone has ever paid more attention to anything than me carrying those egg boxes, each carefully labelled with the varieties of potato within: spill them now and I'd lose any idea of what they are, when they mature, and how best we might enjoy them. It's later than I normally plant them, but the soil and the weather are the boss: it's been too wet and too cold.

I thought I was only planting; it turns out I was harvesting too. In exactly the spot I planned to sow potatoes, my copper trowel found – if not exactly gold – burnished Caramac.[1] A couple of metres away, the neighbouring bed was home last year to *Apios americana*. I say 'was': I left them to overwinter, that they might multiply over summer, giving me plenty to eat and more to plant next year.

So friable is the compost in this raised bed – one I built 18 months ago from a storm-fallen Monterey cypress just a few postcodes away – that the Apios' roots could push through it as easily as fingers into a bath of feathers.

Under the surface, strings of oval tubers, 5cm (2in) or so in diameter, grew: they have a nutty flavour somewhere between Jerusalem artichokes and sweet potatoes. I love them. You can harvest whenever you like from late summer, but if you wait until the cricket season is over and the football well underway, the plant will be preparing for – or even in – dormancy, and be less disturbed by an inquisitive hand.

---

1 There is no other word for that particular golden beige than that of the chocolate bar, alas no longer made.

I've no idea why so few grow Apios.[2] Perennial (buy them once and you have them for life), delicious, unavailable in the shops, beautiful, largely untroubled by pests; instead, we grow what we can already buy. Of course, homegrown potatoes – earlies at least – are a different world to those in the shops, but we dedicate so much of our edible gardens to the most widely and cheaply available, most disease-prone food, missing opportunities to widen our culinary and horticultural larder. It's so easy to be a tribute band, playing songs we already know, when so much deliciousness – and the cultural connection that comes with – is out there to enjoy.

I'm not saying we shouldn't grow the best of the familiar – here I am planting potatoes after all – but let's make room for the lesser known too.

Apios grow beautifully. In midsummer, their winding tendrils cling to and scale long canes; they might make 2 metres or more. By the height of summer, flowers – the peculiar burgundy so common in the '80s[3] and so absent since – dot its height, held at distance as if they think they're too regal to be in the leaves' company.

While that's going on, strings of tubers form unseen, plumping up late in the growing year once they've reached their available wingspan.

The tubers that encroached into my intended potato patch will be replanted elsewhere, or perhaps washed, sliced and fried in olive oil to go with tomorrow's match.

As luck would have it, Apios is a nitrogen fixer, taking nitrogen out of the air and making it available to the soil via its roots, enriching the bed as it grows. The hungry, developing potato plants will happily mop up the extra nutrients and grow more enthusiastically as a result.

Funny to think that these Apios tubers will, in effect, feed us twice.

After this, the sun lost its focus, the clouds fell in and the radiators clanked and creaked into action. Never mind the asparagus supper I'd been dreaming of this morning, it's an evening for heartiness.

---

2 Is it that we are inherently safe when it comes to food, perhaps combined with nurseries preferring you to buy annuals rather than perennials, so you have to come back every year?
3 Especially in Sta Prest trousers of the early '80s Mod revival, and raspberry-flavoured instant desserts such as Angel Delight.

I promise I don't live off gratins, despite their repeated appearance in this book. This is the cheesiest I'm sharing[4] – when the days bring sun and the evenings shudder, I so often want creamy vegetables and something succulent and squeaky to go with. This is a very different sort of gratin to the others, and perfect for when winter is changing places with another season.

It is, by some distance, the best way I know with cardoons. If you grow – or have seen – a globe artichoke plant with somewhat small and disappointingly sized artichokes, chances are it's a cardoon. They are virtually indistinguishable in every other way.

With cardoons, it is the offshoots or hearts you're after. The stalks are celery-like in form, with a flavour between artichoke hearts and chicory. Wear gloves when preparing them: the tannins leave your hands like you've had a decade on the Woodbines.

To prepare cardoons, split each heart into ribbed stems like glaucous celery, top and tail, and thoroughly wash them. You may also need to escort a number of woodlice off the premises. Remove the leaves and use a sharp peeler to shave the ribs from each stem.

This recipe will happily turn to chicory, purple-sprouting or radicchio, and if you use cauliflower it makes for a superb cauliflower cheese.

4 Caveats apply.

Cardoon gratin

SERVES 4

3 x 20cm (8in) cardoon hearts, stems chopped into 7cm (2¾in) pieces
30g (1oz) butter
30g (1oz) plain (all-purpose) flour
300ml (10fl oz) milk
100ml (3½fl oz) double (heavy) cream
15cm (6in) rosemary stem, leaves only, finely chopped
nutmeg
100g (3½oz) grated Gruyère
½–1 tsp chilli (red pepper) flakes
sea salt and freshly ground black pepper

Preheat the oven to 200°C/180°C fan/400°F.

Bring a pan of salted water to the boil. Add the cardoons and simmer for 40–50 minutes until they readily take the point of a knife. Drain, keeping around 200ml (7fl oz) of the cooking liquid. Place the cardoons in a good-sized baking dish: mine is around 26cm (10in) in diameter.

In a small pan, melt the butter and whisk together with the flour over a medium heat for a couple of minutes until it bubbles. Little by little, whisk in the milk until fully incorporated, then whisk in the cooking liquid and cream. Cook for 5 minutes until smooth and thick, stirring often, ideally accompanied by blackbird song.

Add the rosemary, a generous scratching of nutmeg, and season well with salt and pepper.

Pour the sauce over the cardoons, scatter with the grated cheese and cook in the oven until golden – about 20 minutes. Allow to rest for a few minutes before sprinkling with chilli flakes and serving with little gems sliced into wedges.

Mugolio, cedar cones, Mr Whippy and The Gherkin

The horse chestnuts are waving their wet Mr Whippy flowers in the sun. The wind flicks the first loosening petals over the wilting three-cornered leeks beneath. A cheeky pup runs towards me, then spins as if on elastic, back from where he came.

After twenty-one hours of drizzle, the hills lost to a sky of cotton wool, the sun is shooting hard and low across the bay. I have an hour now – maybe two – to find pine cones before the cold of evening takes over.

At the weekend, I tasted mugolio for the first time.[1] I knew of it, and had been encouraged to make some by my foraging friend Liz, but somehow it took until a couple of days ago for that small part of my culinary picture to be coloured in. It is an extraordinary thing – a syrup derived from nothing more complicated than allowing pine, cedar, larch or spruce cones[2] to ferment in an equal weight of sugar. Sweet, resinous and oddly spicy (imagine nutmeg, hazelnut and caramel crossed with a freshly tarred road), I thought immediately of drizzling it over the cheap, yellow vanilla ice cream of my childhood… or waffles (in which ordinarily I have little interest)… or whether it might make the best or worst of mojitos.

My wife and I walked an imaginary dog[3] around the grounds of the now-defunct council offices. Part of the rich diversity of substantial trees that give this place the status of an arboretum town, these grounds have so much to explore. A grand mulberry brought me here – Tupperware in hand – a few summers ago, and every time I come back I find another reason to enjoy it. Today, the handful of Scots pines I was hopeful of carried both young male flowers and a few female flowers, but it was seemingly too early for cones. I wondered if I might have to get in the car and go further afield.

On the way back, a single coniferous tree. My phone[4] told me it was Himalayan cedar, or deodar cedar (*Cedrus deodara*), the national tree of Pakistan. It is a most beautiful thing: deodar means 'wood of the Gods', and it's hard to argue. The tips of a few of the lower branches were just about graspable by the outstretched hand of this enthusiastic lank

---

1 Courtesy of the excellent Colin at the Ground Up Cookery School, who gave me a bottle of two-year-old mugolio.
2 Of all the coniferous trees, ensure you avoid the toxic yew.
3 The unimaginary one has developed a limp that seems to vanish every time someone starts cooking.
4 The 'Picture This' app, worth every penny of its subscription.

on tiptoes; the branches bent pleasingly to a little persuasion, and recoiled even more pleasingly when let go.

Oval cones dotted the upper surface of the branches along their length; a cluster of three then nothing for a metre, or semi-evenly spaced here and there, with no obvious reason as to why. I snapped them off wherever I found them; a punnet of pistachio-coloured cones, each shaped like The Gherkin and perfectly tessellated in soft diamonds that in time, I imagine, break into scales. A little research tells me that these are male cones: deodar cedars carry males on the lower branches of the tree, with the wind blowing their pollen to the female cones in the upper. In time, the grey/green cones grow from their current 2–3cm (1in) to perhaps four times that, turning brown and woody as they mature.

The colour and symmetry of these lovely boys, falling into the container lit up by the surprisingly warm sun, rescued another largely drizzly day.

Mugolio

Scarcely a recipe, this delight is as simple as it gets. Just layer an equal weight of washed cones with sugar – I went for a mix of dark and light soft brown sugars – and leave well alone to ferment. As chance would have it, I picked exactly 300g (10oz) of cones. Use unripe cones in spring and early summer only. You shouldn't need gloves for picking but as soon as you wash them the cones exude just enough resin to remind you of the last time you tried repairing a bicycle tyre.

Leave the jar somewhere sunny to ferment for 30 days. After 7–10 days, the cones release enough liquid to combine with the sugar as fermentation gets underway; pop the lid once a day after this to allow any carbon dioxide to escape. Shake the jar once in a while to encourage the sugar to dissolve. While the pH and sugar creates an environment that ensures there's little danger of harmful bacteria proliferating, it's common to simmer the syrup, cones and all, to dissolve the sugar, improve the texture and enrich the flavour a little at the end of the fermentation. Strain, discarding the cones, and bottle.

Store in the fridge for maximum lifespan (indefinite) and go and buy some cheap vanilla ice cream.

Gorse flowers, a cirl bunting, Rupert Holmes and a piña colada

A few years ago, when life was less than excellent, a particular walk helped me retain balance. What starts as dark, looming conifers, eases into deciduous; the claustrophobic height and adjacency imperceptibly dropping to something relatable, lighter, more relaxed and human.[1] Where the trees thin, bluebells and cow parsley run away from my feet, a path worn here and there by animals making their nocturnal who-knows-why way to who-knows-where. A single wild apple pops blossom towards the sun, the bird chorus becomes more identifiable: the bicycle pump song of the great tit, the chiffchaff – perfectly named after its tune – and the babbling brook of a singing blackbird. At the hedged divide of grazed and ungrazed, an unknown song. The Merlin app tells me I heard – for the first time in my life – a cirl bunting, a rare species making noisy hay in the limited patch it calls home in the UK.

Here, on the mudstone over sandstone, where the dry sandy soils and southerly aspect come together, gorse thrives and with it a surprising number of grateful species. Gorse might not look like a rich habitat, but its spikiness makes it impenetrable to humans; it's a refuge for creatures feathered and furred. Right now, showered in yellow flowers, it is alive with bees and other pollinators in search of nectar. Unseen as they may be on this bright May morning, moth and butterfly larvae make their home.

Gorse's yellow flowers, stark against the blue sky, are not only full of nectar, they're rich in coconut scent. I've intended to pick them in the past but maybe I needed a recipe, a punchline, a point, to finally bring me here, tub in hand.

Today is warm and sunny – an overdue upgrade on spring so far. Bees are alive to the gorse – at 16°C the pollen flies, and with it a more intense coconut scent that attracts both the winged and the two-legged. It takes 30 slow minutes to pick enough of these small yellow flowers to amount to perhaps four decent handfuls. It is half an hour well spent. There is no rushing: you have to proceed relatively slowly to avoid spiking yourself silly, but it is in the settling into a slow meditative plucking that your mind might empty enough to not anticipate conversations with those who wonder what you are up to, to not throw your

---

1 It's only in writing this that the metaphor for the process the walk helped with becomes clear.

thoughts ahead to whatever you'll do when you leave, where – if you are lucky – you'll become a simple, uncomplicated creature, with a mind untroubled by anything other than what you are doing in that moment. England in May, when the clouds part and the rain waits, is hard to beat. I hum Van's 'Warm Love'.

Gorse flower rum

This couldn't be simpler.

MAKES 600ML (1 PINT)

1cm (½in) white caster (superfine) sugar
600ml (1 pint) white rum
2 large handfuls of gorse flowers

Pour the sugar into a jar that will hold at least 750ml (1¼ pints), add 100ml (3½fl oz) of the rum and stir until the sugar has dissolved. Add the gorse flowers and the rest of the rum, pop on the lid and shake/invert the jar to mix. Allow to infuse for 2 days, strain and pour into a sterilised bottle.

Gorse flower syrup

The classic syrup recipe – a little more sugar to water by weight – is tweaked only in allowing this to get just-warm before adding the flowers, as their flavour is easily lost to heat. Try this with sparkling water, Prosecco or in a Tom Collins, with equal parts gin and lemon juice.

MAKES ABOUT 600ML (1 PINT)

150g (5oz) boiling water
500g (1lb 2oz) caster (superfine) sugar
250g cold water
2 handfuls of gorse flowers

Stir the boiling water into the sugar until it has dissolved. Add the cold water, along with the gorse flowers and allow to infuse for 2–3 hours only, then strain and pour into a sterilised bottle.

The Rupert Holmes, aka gorse flower piña colada

Rupert Holmes' anthem of the '70s 'Escape' (aka The Piña Colada Song) is an earworm not easily dislodged. It tells the tale of a bored husband who responds to a personal ad and, well, you can probably guess the rest. It is a piece of cheese larger than anything you'll find in Wallace's fridge, but it brought that pleasingly tropical cocktail to my attention. The coconut triple is spot on here; the lime is an optional tweak to bring a little edge should the pineapple juice be on the sweet side.

SERVES 1

50ml (2fl oz) gorse flower rum
60ml (2¼fl oz) fresh pineapple juice
40ml (1½fl oz) gorse flower syrup
50ml (2fl oz) coconut milk
ice
a squeeze of lime (optional)

Place all but the lime juice in a cocktail shaker and shake like billy-o for a minute or so to incorporate fully.[2] Taste and add a little lime juice if needed. Drink ahead of 'making love at midnight, in the dunes on the cape'.[3]

2 Use a robust glass with your hand over the top, if needs be.
3 Other venues are available.

Broad bean leaves, excellent risotto, being English and Pepsi

Twenty years ago, when the world seemed less bananas, I took a familiar favourite route through Worth Matravers, a beautiful village in Dorset, towards the coast and the almost perfect circle of Chapman's Pool. Somewhere between the two, the path crossed the only field of broad beans in flower I've ever seen.

The sun, unusually hot and hard so early, lifted their scent into the air. It was a perfect moment. Everything made sense. If I hadn't been so regrettably English, I might've laid down on the soil and lost myself to it completely. Instead, I knelt, pushed my face close to their everyday, remarkable blossom, and took in all I could. Every May, when it is still and the morning is shifting sharply from chilly to hot, I kneel by the few plants in the garden and get a glimpse of that Dorset morning, as sure as a sip of Lucozade transports me to the poor timing of being half-term ill.

It's too early for beans – the flowers will eventually develop into those lolloping pods – but even if this was it, even if the pods didn't materialise, I'd grow broad beans. Partly for this scent, but as much for the leaves – every bit the beans' equal – which almost no one eats.

Pluck a soft side branch downwards and it'll shear pleasingly from the stem; taste a young leaf and you'll find it a perfect, fresh, halfway house between broad beans and fresh peas. Just as they are, early and succulent, they're one of the very best salad leaves.

I rarely sow broad beans in early winter in the hope of gaining a few weeks on a spring-sown harvest, but it is one of the markers of my wife's garden year; however inclement, she'll find an ok day six weeks or so before Christmas to push Aquadulce seeds[1] knuckle deep into the soil, in hope rather than expectation that molluscs will sidestep their emerging shoots.

This morning's scent reminds me to sow a late spring batch that will hopefully give me late beans, but most certainly provide summer leaves. Bunyard's Exhibition and a

1 The best for early sowing.

crimson-flowered variety like Grano Violetto are what I turn to in spring, starting them off in toilet roll inners or root trainers to allow them the long root run they favour.

As the flowers wilt, I snip off the top growth of each stem. This directs the plant energy to the developing beans, it removes aphids' favourite place to proliferate, and, stir-fried or shredded into a leafy salad, they are a joy to eat.

This pretty much sums up the pleasure of tending a little patch of the planet: you think you are doing it for one reason, and you haven't the faintest idea of the breadth of reward coming your way.

Broad bean leaf and lemon risotto

I had pretty much given up on risotto[2] until an accidental day in Raymond Blanc's company – a story for another time. Now, as with Pepsi and 'Mr Blue Sky', risotto is a pleasure I desire a few times a year, when I will dedicate myself to its excellence.

Risotto is, like soup, so easy to consign to carelessness – a repository for slack vegetables and half-hearted attention. Constant, mindful stirring in the early stages, excellent stock, allowing the liquid to be incorporated before adding the next ladleful, the resting, and deploying Parmesan in two increments make all the difference between slurry and satisfaction.

Risotto should move when you tip the bowl; add a little more stock or water late on if needed.

2 I mostly prefer textural variation.

SERVES 4

80g (3oz) butter
1 tbsp olive oil
1 shallot, very finely diced
2 celery sticks, very finely diced
350g (12oz) risotto rice
175ml (6fl oz) dry white wine/cider
1 lemongrass stalk
1.2 litres (2 pints) hot vegetable stock
12 broad bean branches, leaves only, finely shredded
½ lemon, pith and pips removed and discarded, flesh thinly sliced
80g (3oz) Parmesan, grated
grated zest of 1 lemon
sea salt and freshly ground black pepper

Add 20g (¾oz) of the butter and the olive oil to a large, heavy-based pan over a medium heat. Add the shallot and celery and cook for 10 minutes until soft and translucent.

Stir in the rice and ½ teaspoon of salt, turning the heat up slightly and stirring for a minute to toast and coat the grains. Add the wine/cider and the lemongrass and cook while stirring until all the liquid has evaporated.

Reduce the heat to medium and add the first ladleful of stock. Stir continuously until all the liquid has evaporated. Repeat with another ladleful of stock, stirring until evaporated. Continue to add a ladleful at a time, stirring constantly, until all the stock is used up.

After 10 minutes of cooking, stir in the broad bean leaves and the lemon slices.

Check the rice after another 5 minutes; you want the grains to be tender but with a little bite. When the rice is ready, remove from the heat, and beat in the remaining butter and half the Parmesan. Check the seasoning, cover and allow it to rest for 2 minutes.

Serve topped with the remaining Parmesan, the lemon zest and a few broad bean flowers if you have them.

Elderflower, a very large sheet of aluminium, Roy Scheider and an excellent martini

Somewhere high in the sky, someone is wobbling a very large sheet of aluminium. Mid-morning, the weight of the air changes and everything switches focus: the gentle swish of the upper branches and birdsong come to the fore, and everything else quietens.[1] A warm welcome wind runs up the valley like a tide looking for its source.

The local park – a two-mile, treed network of meadows, community orchard and grass, with the scurrying River Sid stitching it together – is almost always dotted with idlers, dog walkers and runners grateful for its company. This is where I pick lime flowers in July, keep an eye out for kingfishers and the occasional otter and fill seemingly endless bags with excrement, courtesy of a four-legged companion affectionately, yet understandably, known as Shitbag.

On a whim, I rerouted to the park, taking a chance that the intensity of the air would have the elderflower singing. I could smell it before I saw it, before my feet touched the bridge over which it hung.

Is there a more glorious sight in May – from just far enough away that you can be sure – than an elder covered in scrunched-hanky flowerheads, dozens within tiptoed reach?

Bagless, I tie my shirt at the cuffs, tuck the collar into the knot, and in three short minutes fill the makeshift bag with bold, upright heads. A minute into the two-minute drive back to the house, I wind the window down, so heady is their scent. Thirty seconds after walking through the door, they are in gin, for 100 minutes only, to release the essence of May into the booze as the heavens opened.

1 Very much like that classic beach scene in *Jaws*, when Roy Scheider realises something is happening in the water and the camera foreshortens to bring Scheider up close.

Elderflower gin

This is just gin and elderflower, and as much as it is so simple as to barely deserve the term 'recipe', the specificity of the steps is what delivers perfection.

The elderflower must be alight with its fragrance; a sunny or barometrically intense day is vital.

Pour a litre (1¾ pints) of gin into a shallow dish – this allows a wide area for the flowers to sit in – and place the elderflowers flower-side down in the liquid. Don't snip the flowers from the stems, as the cuts leak bitterness into the gin.

Allow 90–120 minutes, tasting at 80 minutes and removing the flowerheads as soon as the flavour has passed into the gin. You are after the critical point at which the essence of the flowers has fallen into the gin, before any bitterness from the stems soaks out.

Lift the flowerheads out, place a colander underneath and allow them to drip into the dish. Funnel the gin into a bottle and wait for a sunny evening to enjoy with tonic, or in the martini below.

Elderflower martini

My old friend Valentine Warner asserts that a good martini should be an elegant brick thrown through the window of your day. Bravo. Drink one where you want to relax; drink two where you want to sleep.

SERVES 1

80ml (3fl oz) elderflower gin
20ml (¾fl oz) dry white vermouth[2]
ice

Pour the gin and vermouth into a cocktail shaker and add a handful of ice. Shake for 30 seconds. Pour into a chilled glass and enjoy it somewhere you can hear birds singing.

2 Schofield's English Dry Vermouth, from Asterley Brothers, is just perfect.

The best elderflower cordial

Elderflowers need warmth in the wild but not in the kitchen – this is the best elderflower cordial I've ever made, and it's only the sugar syrup that gets hot. I've been making elderflower cordial for a long time, and if you throw it together, stirring everything as it warms in a pan it's pretty grand; if you tweak and care about the seemingly tiny details it becomes something truly special.

MAKES ABOUT 2.5 LITRES (4½ PINTS)

24 good-sized elderflower heads
finely grated zest and juice of 4 lemons
900g (2lb) caster (superfine) sugar

Pick the flowers while the sun is shining on them.

Strip the florets from the stems using a fork and add to a bowl with the finely grated lemon zest. Pour in 1 litre (1¾ pints) of cold water and press the flowers and zest down into it. Place a plate on top and allow to infuse for 8 hours or so.

Dissolve the sugar in 500ml (18fl oz) boiling water, stirring until completely dissolved – it'll take on the consistency of gin that's glassy from the freezer. Allow to cool.

Strain the elderflower liquid into a bowl, add the sugar syrup and the lemon juice and stir together.

Behold, a miracle: clean, utterly bright, delicious spring-into-summer in a bottle.

Dilute to taste with water, gin, fizz…

Globe artichokes, Chuck Berry, saving a few quid and vignarola

He was found on the third stair of the council house where he'd spent the second half of his life and I the first third of mine. Had his beloved cat brushed past in search of a tea yet to be put out, it might've been enough to take him over the tipping point at which he would've pitched forward on to his nose, not that it would've hurt; it was too late for that.

The date of that cool, late May day falls in spring; his birthday almost three weeks later is very definitely summer – somewhere between these anniversaries I make vignarola. I don't make it for him – a delicate Roman stew of the best of the changing seasons might be as far from his ideal supper as a skip is from a raspberry – but one way or another, he often appears at my shoulder when I'm making it.

A quarter of a century gone, I might be feeling a little guilty – as I am this week – at not yet placing pointless flowers on his grave while not quite being able to stop myself having a pointless conversation with someone who isn't there, and mostly never really quite was.

As I pod the beans, I almost always smile that the potent combination of cigarettes and unhappiness took him before I'd solved the riddle of what I might get him for his 65th. A few quid saved: he'd have liked that.

I only make vignarola in this season-switching window: towards the end of the asparagus, the first broad beans and peas, the smallest of artichokes, mint and chives from the cutting back of the herbs before they get too leggy, and the pleasure of spring onions doubled if I've remembered to sow them for an early return.

Today, I make it while listening to Chuck Berry's 'Nadine', which no matter how many times he played it, he couldn't help himself saying 'listen to those saxophones son, aren't they great?' And every time they were.

Vignarola

I make this differently every time, using the proportions below. This year, the peas are behind thanks to the lack of sunshine, so I used frozen – 250g (9oz) – as I wanted to make this before mid-June approached.

The difference between good and exceptional is made as much as anything by cooking each vegetable for just long enough to be perfect; the asparagus should retain resistance and taste slightly of unsalted peanuts, and so on.

By all means, use different herbs – I choose mint, parsley and chives, as (along with the lemon) they keep everything bright and clear, but lovage, basil and so on work differently well.

Preparing the artichokes is simple, though do clear the table ahead: preparing or eating globe artichokes is one of the few times you end up with more than you started with.

SERVES 4

8–12 small artichokes
juice of 1 lemon and finely grated zest of half
4 tbsp olive oil, plus a little to finish
8 spring onions (scallions)
2 heads of wet garlic,[1] or 2 garlic cloves, finely chopped
220ml (8fl oz) white wine or cider
600g (1lb 5oz) broad beans weighed in their pods, beans only
250g (9oz) asparagus, tough bases discarded, roughly chopped
600g (1lb 5oz) fresh peas weighed in their pods, peas only
salt and pepper
small handful of mint, chopped
small handful of flat-leaf parsley, chopped
small handful of chives, chopped, plus a couple of chive flowers if you have them
sea salt and freshly ground black pepper

First prepare the artichokes. Slice off the top third and stem, pull the tough outer leaves off and trim the stub of the stem to remove the rough outer. Slice lengthways in half and drop into cold water acidulated with the lemon juice, to prevent the artichokes discolouring.

---

1 Wet garlic, sometimes known as green garlic, is the immature garlic bulb and edible green stalk available at this time of year.

Heat the olive oil in a pan and cook the spring onions and garlic over a medium heat, stirring frequently, until soft. Add the wine and an equivalent amount of water.[2]

Bring to a simmer, add the artichoke halves and season well. Cover and cook for 15 minutes, stirring occasionally. Test the artichokes for tenderness – allowing a little longer if needed. Add the broad beans and asparagus and cook for another couple of minutes with the lid on, then add the peas, cooking for just another 2 minutes. Season to taste.

Ladle into bowls and sprinkle with the lemon zest. Serve warm, scattered with the herbs (and flowers) and drizzled lightly with olive oil, with Chuck Berry on in the background.

2 Don't be tempted to add more; the vegetables should be sitting not entirely in the liquid rather than swimming.

Football rattles, apricots, sparrowhawks and a gooseberry and elderflower shrub

The magpies have brought their football rattles, and rather than one for sorrow or three for a girl, they now more commonly line up in two-for-joy or four-for-a-boy gaggles.

They're high in the neighbour's dead tree, or on a telegraph pole; anywhere they can look down on the hedges. They're here for the baby sparrows, the young blackbirds and other small birds. And I don't like it.

I'm in the garden checking on the four fruits hanging on the dwarf apricot. It might not sound like much, but they are the first that the pollinators have worked their magic to create. I'm not naive enough to imagine the fruit will cling on for the summer – the tree's young years will find them too much of a burden even for so few – but it means next year carries a racing chance that midsummer will bring apricots.

I grew apricots back at the farm. While they lack the lush succulence of a peach that leaves the tree without persuasion, a fresh apricot – plucked after a day of sunshine on its back – has a rich, buttery intensity that lifts the soul. So, even in this small garden, I can't not find space for a single, self-fertile, dwarf apricot tree. These few fruit mean it is slowly putting down roots, fuelled by the occasional liquid feed and a great deal of hope.

This morning is one of small jobs, easily overlooked. As well as dreaming of apricots, I'm cutting back the chives (their flowers are going over, the leaves becoming coarse), twisting off sweet cicely seeds before they become tough, picking pink gooseberries, sieving and simmering the mugolio (page 103) that's been quietly fermenting this last month, and whatever else guilts me into being done.

All the time, that rattle fills the high air.

Sitting with a coffee, still for a few moments, I remember reading that magpies mate for life. Hence, I guess, 'one for sorrow, two for joy'. Maybe that explains why they're here most often in even numbers at the moment – joy, boy, gold – one of each couple searches for food for them both, while the other keeps dixie.

It occurs to me that I excitedly told half the world when a sparrowhawk took a pigeon from its path not six feet from my head, the only sound breaking the warm evening silence a single percussive WHOMPH. That was okay. I did like that. I felt like I'd been allowed into a parallel world, like two bubbles from a child's toy momentarily touching before floating on their way. This goes on all the time, I just don't see it.

A sparrowhawk is 'wild', a magpie 'more cunning than the raven', the knower and bearer of good news and bad; they know when we're going to die and how we are born, we are told, and so their presence unsettles. Yet not everywhere: in France they are loved – their call taken as an ancient warning of predators approaching; in China they are seen as bringers of good fortune; in Korea they are admired and welcomed. And so it goes.

So as much as I may be unsettled by old stories frequently told, I will try to welcome the magpie as much as the sparrowhawk that was sat on the telegraph pole eyeing up the pigeons cooing at two-a-penny yesterday afternoon, and as much as the owl that calls long and loud into the night.

Sweet cicely apricots, yoghurt and mugolio

Until the sweet day when the garden provides, apricots must be bought. In the time since I ate a homegrown one, I've managed to convince myself that shop-bought apricots are as excellent as homegrown – they certainly taste it today – but I know next summer will tell me otherwise. Get lucky and they really can be exceptional – quite luscious enough to eat as they are, they have so much to give with a little heat to replace the sunshine they missed by being picked a little early to travel.

Halved, stoned and gently roasted, their flavour intensifies and the texture surrenders, but if the oven's not on anyway, I cook them in a pan with a little butter. Just be careful; they scorch easily.

SERVES 4

40g (1½oz) nuts and seeds[1]
40g (1½oz) butter
400g (14oz) apricots – around 10–12, halved and stoned
generous pinch of ground cardamom
plain yoghurt
about half a dozen sweet cicely seeds or 1 tsp fennel seeds, roughly chopped
4 tbsp mugolio (page 103) or honey

Over a medium heat, toast the seeds and nuts in a dry frying pan that's large enough to accommodate the apricot halves without crowding, shaking the pan to prevent the seeds and nuts burning. When lightly toasted, tip into a bowl.

Place the butter in the frying pan and, once it is gently fizzing, add the apricots, cut side down, and cook until just beginning to catch and colour. Turn the halves over and lower the heat just a touch, lightly pressing on the cut side with a spatula to flatten the dome of each apricot half a little against the pan.

Sprinkle ground cardamom on the cut side of each apricot half. Once the undersides start to soften and colour, flip the apricots on to the cut side again, turn the heat up a little and allow to cook a minute or two longer.

Spoon yoghurt into each bowl,[2] add your apricot halves, sprinkle with the seeds/nuts and sweet cicely and drizzle with mugolio or honey.

Gooseberry and elderflower shrub

A shrub – from the Arabic *shurb* meaning 'to drink' – is a lively, fermented coming together of vinegar, sugar and fruit and either drunk as is (for the sour-dedicated), or diluted (1 part shrub to 5 parts diluter is a good ratio to start with). They can be very fine snuck into a cocktail.

These sweet-sharp drinking vinegars are as delicious as they are good for you, and once you have the rough template you can play with whatever flavours you fancy. The core recipe is simple: crush your fruit and combine with sugar, allow to ferment for 24 hours or so at room temperature, then add vinegar and allow to mature for 7–14 days, tasting

---

1 I went with rough thirds of sunflower seeds, pumpkin seeds and broken-up walnuts.
2 I find that some like fruit with their yoghurt, others yoghurt with their fruit, hence no quantities given here.

every now and again after a week. My default ratio is 4 parts sugar to 5 of vinegar, though this recipe has a little more sugar thanks to the sharpness of the gooseberries.

The red colour here is due to me using red gooseberries.

MAKES ABOUT 300ML (10FL OZ)

200g (7oz) caster (superfine) sugar
250g (9oz) gooseberries, top and tailed and crushed (I whizzed mine very briefly in a blender)
240ml (8fl oz) cider vinegar
1 lemongrass stalk, outer skin removed
100ml (3½fl oz) elderflower cordial

Stir the sugar and gooseberries together in a bowl, cover with a tea towel and leave to ferment on the side for 36 hours or so.

Warm the vinegar in a pan over a low heat, stirring frequently. Bash the lemongrass lightly with a rolling pin to release the flavour and scent. Place it and the gooseberries in a jar and pour the warm vinegar over it. Allow to cool and stir in the cordial. Leave it to infuse for at least 24 hours.

Pour through a strainer into a jug and decant into a sterilised jar or bottle. You can use it immediately, but it's better off left to mature for a week in the fridge. It will last for 3 weeks or so in the fridge.

Gooseberry and elderflower shrub G&T

Take the recipe for this sunny evening attitude adjuster as the starting point from which to play – you might need a little more or less shrub, or prefer a touch more tonic, depending on the strength of the shrub and your tastes.

SERVES 1

50ml (2fl oz) gin
50ml (2fl oz) gooseberry and elderflower shrub
50ml (2fl oz) tonic
a wedge of lime, squeezed into and then dropped into the glass
plenty of ice

You don't need instructions.

Cherries, walnut leaves, gilets and clafoutis

Nobody knows what the fuck to wear. On the walk with the hound, I see sun hats, trench coats, gilets, T-shirts, woolly hats, shorts, scarves and sandals. The only thing we all know for certain, is that at some point today we will be too hot for our clothes or cold to the bone, and very likely both.

I'm waiting. My body needs June and September; when you have skin the colour of supermarket shortcrust, you can live without July and August, but not its shoulders. A combination of April and October have taken June's place, and my body and soul feels its absence.

On the way home, I notice that the elders have pushed their flowers further from the leaves as if they've had enough of them; their scent is heavier than May's, like warm elderflower cordial made with someone else's pee. It's too early for green walnuts – mid July is usual – and chances are they will be later this year, but in checking on the tree by the river, their spicy, sherbetty leaves brighten my fingers with very possibly my favourite leaf scent of all.

Luckily, the greengrocer came to the rescue. Somewhere in Kent, the earliest cherries in the sunniest locations are being harvested, and despite a bag of greedy handfuls tipping the scales at £12 odd, I couldn't care less: they bring deep purple sunshine. I make clafoutis and eat too many fresh from the colander as the rain falls.

From the window, I can see in the garden that the Babington's leek heads are opening, the first colour blushes the mirabelles, and the bush roses are catching up with the rambler that flourishes across the garage. And I wait, and I wait some more, for June to arrive on the southwesterly that makes all of it sway.

Cherry and coriander seed clafoutis

A decade ago, we stayed with friends in Aquitaine, just as the early strawberries gave way to cherries in the market. We had no need of them: cherries hung from the tree outside their house at just a height where I could pull the most abundant branches down for my daughter to pick, open-eyed at the pleasure of each. A special cherry is a reason to be alive, but if, like me, you buy more than you can eat fresh, or if they are good but not that good, clafoutis is about the best way with them.

You might be thinking 'coriander?' but trust me. Coriander seed shares a compound with blueberries and they go surprisingly well together; I wondered if coriander and cherries might make a happy marriage too, and I'm very, very glad I wondered. Despite sprinkling a considerable amount of only briefly pounded coriander seed over the finished clafoutis, it tastes not of coriander but the cherries taste even more of themselves. Trust me, I'm a doctor.[1]

For those who might be interested, I've made this with gluten-free flour, oat milk and oat cream (omitting the butter), and though slightly different and a touch oatier in flavour, it is equally good to a dairy version.

SERVES 6

100g (3½oz) plain (all-purpose) flour, plus a little for dusting
pinch of salt
1 tsp vanilla extract or seeds from a vanilla pod
250ml (9fl oz) whole milk
3 eggs
60g (2¼oz) caster (superfine) sugar
120ml (4fl oz) double (heavy) cream, plus more to serve
350g (12oz) cherries, stalk and stone removed
20g (¾oz) unsalted butter, cut into small cubes, plus a little for greasing the dish
1 tbsp icing (confectioner's) sugar
1 tsp coriander seeds, crushed in a mortar and pestle

Preheat the oven to 230°C/210°C fan/440°F. Grease a round baking dish of around 25cm (10in) diameter, or 28 x 20cm (11 x 8in) if rectangular, and dust it lightly with flour.

---

1 Well, an Honorary Professor of Liverpool University, but still.

Sift the flour and salt into a large bowl. Whisk in the vanilla and half the milk until it forms a smooth batter. Whisk – as quickly as you can – the eggs in one at a time, followed by the caster sugar, the rest of the milk and the cream.

Spread the cherries in the baking dish, pour in the batter and dot the cubes of butter across the top. Place the dish into the oven and cook for 20–25 minutes until plump and golden. Remove from the oven and allow to cool a little, before dusting with icing sugar and sprinkling with the crushed coriander seeds.

Serve warm with double cream.

Pickled cherries

I use this as my core recipe around which the spices vary – the version in my book *Sour* has star anise instead of cinnamon and clove, and black peppercorns in place of white – and you should try that too. The leftover vinegar makes an excellent dressing for salad.

50g (1¾oz) caster (superfine) sugar
500ml (18fl oz) white wine vinegar
1 tsp fennel seeds
1 clove
a 5cm (2in) cinnamon stick
6 white peppercorns
1 bay leaf
350g (12oz) cherries

In a medium pan, bring all but the cherries to a gentle simmer over a medium heat. Stone and halve the cherries over the jar you intend to store them in, to catch every drop of their juice. Place the cherries in the jar, then pour the hot vinegar and spices over them. Seal the jar and allow at least a fortnight for the cherries' flavour to develop – longer if you can.

Summer, waiting for buses, Moroccan mint and shakshuka

And just like that, it happened.

It's been skin-tighteningly hot for a few days in a row, and it's only rained on one of them. I haven't been tempted to light a fire or take a bath just to warm my bones. The grass has its feathers on, the tiniest grasshoppers have arrived, those little shitty aphids are clambering along the upper reaches of the broad beans, and I couldn't be happier to see them.

'June' is finally here, and it's all my fault.

Last week, I drove past the patch of grass where decades ago – under the slightest encouragement from the weather – all the kids on the estate poured out of their homes to play cricket and football. Opposite, a bus shelter of that inverted L design, set at such an angle as to funnel the prevailing wind and all it brought with it directly at those who sought its protection. For three decades one of its four panes of glass was missing, allowing a lazy traveller the opportunity to park an idle backside in its metal frame.

Should you be in a hurry, or be a little bored by the wait, there were two ways to summon a bus: start walking (a double-decker would turn the corner at exactly the point at which you couldn't quite make it back to the bus stop in time to catch it), or light a cigarette. As soon as you drew that first luscious lungful deep into yourself – at precisely the moment a little tickle in your blood told you that the nicotine was racing about your system, turning off the lights of its craving as it went – a bus would loom into view.

In exactly this way, I wrote about June's absence last week and in so doing Sod's-Lawed it into being.[1] Everybody owes me one.

A few of the potato plants have flowers, a glorious sign that below ground tubers are forming. Awful as I am, I couldn't help winkling one or two from a few of the most well-developed plants. Cooked briefly, drained and allowed to sit for a few minutes, lid on, a

---

1 Next week, I'll tackle world peace, great riches and life everlasting.

generous wodge of butter slipping into the two-dimensional along with a few just-picked Moroccan mint leaves, they were every bit as good as anything I've eaten this year.

The first broad beans are picked. With the soil drying, there has been weeding, mulching and a last wave of pea seedlings planted out in the hope they'll avoid the slugs' attentions in the drier weather. It feels like a midsummer, warm-weather Christmas.

Everything feels very different to last week, and I like it very much.

Early summer shakshuka

I eat variations of this all through the year and at any time of day – it's as fine for brunch as it is for supper – and this 'heading into summer' version is a serious joy. While in cooler weather I might include the traditional cumin or other sources of Middle Eastern/North African earthiness, this has just the light, floral touch of coriander seed to complement and brighten, dabs of harissa oil bringing lively punctuation. The weights of beans and peas given is without the pods. And yes, by all means make this with frozen peas and beans if that is what you have to hand. As often as not, I'll fancy the saltiness of feta here, but today I preferred the silk of burrata.

SERVES 4

2 tbsp olive oil
1 onion, finely chopped
2 heads of wet garlic,[2] or 2 garlic cloves, finely chopped
400g (14oz) can chopped tomatoes
300g (10oz) broad beans
300g (10oz) peas
1 tbsp red wine vinegar
4 eggs
ball of burrata, or broken feta if you prefer
2 tsp smoked harissa mixed with 1 tsp water
1 tsp ground coriander
½ small bunch of flat-leaf parsley, roughly chopped
½ small bunch of coriander (cilantro), roughly chopped
sea salt and freshly ground black pepper

2 See page 121.

Warm the olive oil in a frying pan over a medium heat. Add the onion and cook, stirring occasionally, for 10 minutes or so until soft. Add the garlic and cook for another 2 minutes.

Stir in the chopped tomatoes and 200ml (7fl oz) water and simmer for 15 minutes or so, stirring occasionally.

Add the broad beans to a pan of boiling water, simmer for 2 minutes, then add the peas and simmer for another 2 minutes.[3] Drain and add to the tomato sauce. Season with salt and pepper.

The consistency of the sauce should be such that when creating a depression in which to crack each egg, it should only just hold enough of its shape rather than closing over; add a little water should you need to. Stir in the vinegar.

Crack an egg into a cup, and having made a scoop in the sauce with a spoon, lower the egg into it. Repeat with each egg. Cover with a lid and allow to cook until the eggs are as you'd like them – the white should be cooked and the yolk runny after about 5 minutes.

Break the burrata into pieces and dot across the surface, then drizzle with the harissa. Sprinkle with salt, pepper, the ground coriander and the chopped herbs.

Serve with excellent bread or toast.

3 If using frozen beans and peas, count the timing from when the water returns to a simmer.

Plumcots, Lancaster planes, lavender and a very good Eton Mess

I was 17 and in my mum's front room, Friday night, the TV on: *Gardeners' World*. Me thinking: 'If this is ever my Friday night, if ever I get into this nonsense, somebody do me in.' The greatest waste of life: people with time and money on their hands creating pretend places rather than getting out into the real ones; making jumbled floral mixtapes of their favourite tracks, and never getting to know the albums they come from and that give them meaning.

And yet here I am.

Eating the first of the fruit the young plumcot[1] has produced reminded me of why I look beyond what the shops have to offer. Why I have a garden. Sweet, rich, luscious and giving, they have just a touch of almond to their flavour that rounds them off perfectly. Let's hope the birds focus elsewhere, that the hornets – the first Lancastered past my ear this afternoon – go after the neighbour's berries instead.

I've been away and come back to a generous clutch of new plants in pots. It feels like Christmas. Someone, clonk me over the head with a shovel.

Skirret, mojito mint, wood sorrel, oca, Japanese wineberry, Serpent garlic, perennial kales and more. Old friends and new.

The garden is calling my name: a few more pieces of the puzzle to slip into place.

It's a peculiar garden. At times I see it as others might – untidy, a compromise of time and desire, immature – but mostly I love every glance from every angle because of what it means, what it gives and what it will be, as much as what it is.

I want it to be as close to a natural coming together of plants as possible – and by that I don't mean their relationship is without a designing hand, or that they are interplanted

---

1 A hybrid of a plum and an apricot with a leaning towards the plum, and yes, there is an aprium that is more apricot, and very good it is too.

slavishly to what might wildly occur – but that they are in balance, requiring little intervention. A little pulling back of this, a pruning of that, a shaping here and there.

Look at the Turkish rocket, flowering high and handsome in yellow; it's encroaching on the Japanese plum. I haven't the enthusiasm to knock it back – the plum can stand it, and the rocket will soon throw seed around and then shrink back a good degree – but where it looms over the daylilies like a bank of Death Eaters, I chop it back a little. This is my kind of gardening.

I never had the heart to eat daylilies when I first grew them. How can you eat a flower that only lasts a day? But it dawned on me that this is the perfect flower to eat, that once it's had most of its day in the sun, it's better to pick and eat it rather than leave it to wither. Will it keep body and soul together? It will not. But it feeds me – and a platoon of beneficial insects – in so many other ways too.

In front of the daylilies, in front of the Turkish rocket, in front of the Japanese plum – the last in a cascade of ever diminishing plants – Cassis Ice chives.

In almost every way no different to a familiar chive; it's just the flowers: more deeply purple, more tightly held perhaps, and – peculiarly – their flavour is delayed, taking a long three seconds of 'these taste of nothing' time until they arrive on your tongue, all lights flashing, in glorious oniony technicolor. Broken into florets and sprinkled over a salad, they bring a really special punchy punctuation.

And just a week later – the time I've been away – they stand heavy with seeds. A little rattle and more will spring to life in the months ahead.

And so in the gaps between deadlines and travelling about, I plant the new arrivals and hope that some, most or all are in the right place. And after this time away, returning frazzled, thinking about where they might go and getting some in the ground has settled me from being a hot air balloon bumping along the ground to one that has come to rest, flame burning again, upright, and facing the right way.

And so here I am. I came for the potatoes and mulberries, and I found a sense of attachment to the planet, a reason to move into the days ahead. I found so much I wasn't expecting. A joke I was let in on. Whatever I needed, growing and cooking food has given in abundance. Writing about it, yet more so.

The seasons have gone from what I saw as cold and wet or hot and dry, to numerous foldings and intersections of the four we are taught; lavender has gone from just 'lavender' to so many subtle and not so subtle variations on a theme. Bright and shade, shadow and light, things moving on whether I'm here to see them or not, flavours I've never tasted until today, changes that make me stop and notice. Now, I have a point.

Gooseberry and strawberry Eton Mess

For a few short weeks gooseberries shake hands with strawberries. Of the many ways of bringing them together, this is as good as I know, elderflower marrying them perfectly.

A tumble of seasonal fruit barely combined with meringue and whipped cream, Eton Mess is not hard to enjoy. The only way to go wrong is to make this too sickly: if the fruity combination is potentially too sweet, a little yoghurt stirred through the cream helps to balance things.

Adding lavender makes such a difference, somehow lightening and deepening the coming together, but don't worry if you have none to hand. In the unlikely event you have any Eton Mess left for the next day, bear in mind the lavender will become more intense in flavour.

I have to tell you I couldn't be arsed to make meringues; my need for the combination of flavours and textures was too urgent.

SERVES 6

300g (10oz) gooseberries, top and tailed
4 tbsp elderflower cordial
400ml (14fl oz) double (heavy) cream
160g (5½oz) yoghurt
240g (8½oz) strawberries, halved or quartered depending on size
10 small (about 10cm/4in) meringues, broken into pieces
drizzle of pomegranate molasses (optional)
2 lavender flowers, florets plucked from the stem (optional)
toasted flaked (slivered) almonds (optional)

Add the gooseberries to a pan just wide enough to take them in a single layer, along with a lick of water just sufficient to reach their circumferences. Over a low-medium heat, cook the gooseberries enough to encourage them to collapse and release their juice. Allow them to cool, then either leave textured or blend until smooth. Stir in the elderflower cordial.

Whip the cream until it holds a floppy quiff. Fold in the yoghurt.

Place the strawberries in a large bowl. Break the meringues into pieces and fold most of them into the yoghurt cream; then stir this into the strawberries until semi-incorporated. Spoon over the gooseberry purée, dot with a little more meringue, zorro with pomegranate molasses (if you like) and sprinkle with lavender flowers and/or flaked almonds.

Serve with a big spoon and see how much people come back for.

Strawberry sorbet

I tend to make this when I have strawberries that are just on the turn, capturing their sweet intensity before they are lost to collapse.

MAKES AROUND 900ML (1½ PINTS)

300g (10½oz) strawberries, halved
300g (10½oz) caster (superfine) sugar
500ml (18fl oz) water
240ml (8fl oz) dryish white wine
50ml (1¾fl oz) lime or lemon juice

Add all but the wine and juice to a pan and bring to the boil, stirring to dissolve the sugar. Simmer for 5 minutes. Swizz in a blender until smooth, then add the wine and blend for a moment to incorporate. Strain through a sieve into a plastic tub and allow to cool.

If using an ice-cream maker, follow the instructions that come with it. Otherwise, freeze for 6 hours or so, or overnight, then transfer the sorbet to a blender and swizz briefly to create a smoother consistency, before freezing once again.

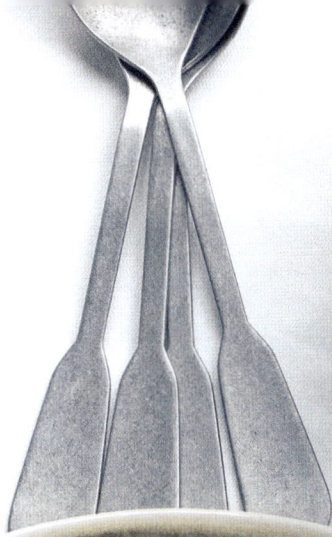

Lime blossom, Charles Trenet, Jon Voight and a summer Tom Collins

A year and two weeks ago, I realised I'd been walking on the wrong side of the river. I'd been doing it for a few mornings before I recognised I was auto-piloting along the side I usually favour least on my morning loop with the hound: perhaps the appeal of a change; maybe to give myself a better chance of coinciding with the man who, long-handled walking poles in hand, sings standards from the '20s, '30s and '40s as he strides towards the sea. 'La Mer' never sounded so good than through tatty willows across the river that splits yet unites this town.

The day I realised I had made a habit of the wrong side, I picked up a faint scent. The next day stronger. One of three smallish lime trees was in flower.[1] Its distance from the path and the cloudiness of the sky diluted its fragrance, but it was there in the air.

A week later and my shoes took me across the usual bridge to my usual side of the river of their own accord. Had they been slip-ons, they might have walked themselves over had my feet stopped.

On a bank a few yards from the path, a huge cathedral of a lime stands regal as if being carried shoulder high to the sea. I walked around it, its branches hanging almost to the ground, swaying in the breeze as if to the theme from *Midnight Cowboy*. The sun now strong, the scent enveloped me. It was like happily drowning in a cloud of lemon honey.

The bees – how many thousands, drawn from how far? – made a huge hum of the tree, their greatest concentration where the sun's spotlight made candles of its flowers. I couldn't escape the enormity that this happens whether I'm here or not. It's too glorious for no one to see it, surely?

I walked to the beach. On the way back, where the sun had moved around the tree, so too the bees. That cloud of lemon honey met my nose: maybe there's a little lemongrass to it, and is that a hint of lime zest? A touch of mint?

---

1 There are three fairly widespread species of lime here in the UK: large-leaved lime, aka broad-leaved lime (*Tilia platyphyllos*), small-leaved lime (*Tilia cordata*) and common lime (*Tilia x europaea*), a natural hybrid of the other two. Common lime grows largest (though you can only tell that if it is at its mature height), is perhaps more easily distinguished from large-leaved lime by the fact that the latter flowers first (usually in June here in the UK), is commonest on chalky ground, and its floppy large leaves darken through summer into autumn. Common lime and small-leaved lime flower in July. Small-leaved lime, a key part of lowland forests in the south of England since the last Ice Age, has the rather pleasing characteristic of its flowers pointing in any direction, rather than hanging elegantly as with other limes. The early spring leaves of the small-leaved lime are particularly good to eat as a salad leaf – succulent, nutty and bright. In all likelihood, this early-flowering lime is a large-leaved lime, which tends to flower first.

And today, a year later, all this is happening again.[2] The limes on one side of the river are just going over while the regal tree is just thinking of firing up. I imagine the bees sat on those willows, serenaded by Mr Walking Poles, wondering whether it's today those flowers will call their name.

And today, I remember that in the old place, when we had bees, the earliest honey of the year was heavy with lime pollen and had a distinctly minty edge, a hint I'd picked up in the flowers' scent.

Somewhere I read that limes are not – as many trees are – wind-pollinated, but that their glorious perfume is what draws the bees to pollinate their flowers. Perhaps before I recognised it, before I consciously picked up the scent on the 'wrong' side of the river, those flowers were calling me, the scent reaching me earlier than I realised; me little more than a six-foot-one bee drawn to the lemon honey.

Lime flower cordial

I wanted to capture that sweet scent of summer – as much of what July is to me now as elderflower is to May – and I wondered if a cordial might work similarly well. How is it even possible to turn a scent into a flavour?

In German and ancient folklore, the lime is the tree of truth,[3] so I know you'll believe me when I tell you that this is at least the equal of elderflower, and I say that not lightly. Seriously, drop everything and make this now, before the flowers go past their peak. If you find a lime whose flowers are over, keep looking for others, as slight variations in location as much as species mean they can be three weeks apart in flowering.

You want open flowers, ideally on the pale side. As with elderflower, a sunny day for picking is best. It's quickest if you pick the flower with its leaf and snip the flowers off when home, and compost the rest.

When I made this last year, I used the juice of 4 lemons, which worked well, but after about a week the acidity faded, so this year I've gone for the juice of 6 lemons.

---

2 Last summer was cool and rainy; everything was late, shunted a fortnight on. This year – despite how it feels right now – most things are as on time as they ever are.

3 Lime is a sacred tree in many cultures – love, fertility and wisdom are all in its power to convey to those that sit in its shade.

MAKES 1 LITRE (1¾ PINTS), PLUS ENOUGH FOR A GLASS TO TRY IT

700g (1½lb) boiling water
700g (1½lb) sugar
juice of 6 lemons
lime flowers – a couple of very large double handfuls is the nearest meaningful measure I can give; I'm sure you get the rough idea.

Pour the boiling water over the sugar, stirring to dissolve it. Allow it to cool, then add the lemon juice. Pour half of the syrup into a jar no smaller than 1.5 litres (3 pints), then add the lime flowers.

Top with the rest of the syrup, leaving an inch or two of space at the top. Take a scrunched sheet of greaseproof paper and place this in the top of the jar to keep the flowers below the surface – this maximises the infusion and prevents them oxidising.

Close the jar and allow to infuse for 36 hours or so. Strain through a sieve and pour into a sterilised bottle. Store in the fridge and it should keep for a month, very possibly much longer. By all means freeze in a tub to keep it for even longer.

A summer Tom Collins

The simplicity of a Tom Collins should not mask its intensity; as perfect a celebration of summer as this may be, it is pretty full on. If you can open your left eye without using your fingers after the first sip, you haven't used enough lemon. If you prefer a longer drink, this is so good stretched out with tonic to taste.

SERVES 1

50ml (2fl oz) gin
50ml (2fl oz) lemon juice
50ml (2fl oz) lime flower cordial
a great deal of crushed ice
wedge of lime

Place all but the lime in a cocktail shaker (or a sturdy glass with your held hand over) and shake for 15 seconds. Pour into a glass, squeeze in the lime wedge and add to the drink. Sit in your favourite place, ideally feet in the sun, head in the shade and contemplate the finer moments of your day, week, life.

15 JULY

Chilean guava, central Bath, survivalists and a rainy day summer soup

There is day in summer where the sea holly turns electric blue, the yellow daylilies catch up with the red, the first broad beans forget to hold themselves away from the horizontal, and the scent of the Chilean guava flowers writes its name across the nostrils of anyone lucky enough to be in their vicinity. It turns out that day was yesterday.

God that scent. I love it even more than the delicious berries, and that is very big talk. It is utterly transporting, giving me nostalgia for places, people and times I've never known.[1] Lighter than elderflower yet of equal depth, it is the imaginary perfume of the imaginary love of your life. It is – like a car park in central Bath – impossible to navigate to by other landmarks. To sit in its company is to be properly alive. Just like a summer cloud, it passes then returns.

As with broad beans and elder, I would grow them for the flowers' perfume alone. I've no idea how a few dozen of the tiny bell flowers on each of four plants can fill the entire garden like the most joyous of scented passenger airbags, but they do.

I spent much of the day on the garden. I moved rocks heavier than I could budge with my bare hands.[2] I dug out high-growing ornamentals of I know not what kind and planted low-growing herbs, skirret, Allium 'Ping Pong', Serpent garlic, some perennial kales, a couple of Nine Star broccolis and an early variety of rhubarb.

The sun tightened my skin and filled me up. It was a very good day.

This morning, as the rain falls hard, my face feels pleasingly slapped and shiny as greaseproof paper, and the rainy window makes a kaleidoscope of the garden. I could be in another country.

It is a soup kind of a day.

---

1 Very much how The Blue Nile remind me of that time I was the victim of unrequited love in a rainy Glasgow, despite not being.
2 I used a metal post to lift the heaviest an inch, then wedged a stone under it, then repeated over a couple of hours until it was excavated and a crucial metre to the side of its original position.

Rainy summer day pea and tarragon soup

Everyone had someone in their class who either is or was a survivalist, someone certain that the end is nigh, and that the thoroughness of their research meant that they and only they would endure the coming apocalypse. This soup is the colour of their many-pocketed jacket, and suits today's weather in inverse proportion to how much that jacket suited its wearer.

Using the pods as well as the peas deepens the flavour, and while you could use parsley and/or lovage here, peas and tarragon is such a wonderful and underused combination, with the mint bringing a touch of bright optimism that a rainy summer day needs.

SERVES 4

500g (1lb 2oz) fresh peas in their pods
1 tbsp olive oil, plus a drizzle to serve
1 shallot, finely chopped
1 large potato (300g/10oz or so), peeled and grated
4 generous sprigs of tarragon, leaves only
1 litre (1¾ pints) vegetable stock
nutmeg
5 fresh mint leaves, thinly sliced
splash of double (heavy) cream
sea salt and freshly ground black pepper

Separate the peas from their pods, then snip off and discard the tough ends and any easily removed stringy bits from the pea pods, and thinly slice the good parts.

Heat the oil in a large pan over a medium heat and fry the shallot for 7–8 minutes until soft and translucent. Add the potato, tarragon, sliced pea pods and the stock and bring to the boil, then lower the heat and simmer for 8 minutes. Add the peas and cook for 2 minutes from the moment the soup returns to a simmer.

Remove from the heat and blend on high until smooth; if fibres survive the blending, pass through a sieve. Season to taste and add a very good grating of nutmeg.

Sprinkle with mint, swirl lightly with cream, a little olive oil and perhaps a touch more pepper and nutmeg. Soft, warm rolls with excellent salty butter would be ideal here.

Fig leaves, Pat Jennings, a baby's scalp and an excellent ice cream

Every time I see a fig leaf I think of Pat Jennings.[1] I was a goalie at primary school and Jennings was one of the best in the world. I liked him even though he and Pat Rice turned up too frequently in the packets of football cards that came with a bubblegum that was the pink of a cat's tongue, giving you swapsies no one else required. There seemed to be three Pat Jennings for every Kevin Hector.

His hair looked like it had been piped on by a chef, the main aim seemingly to form a perfect bell in silhouette and to cover all but the lobes of his ears. This was not his most distinguishing feature: Jennings had huge hands. Famously, he could pick up a football one-handed from above. He played much of his career without gloves, adopting them late and giving his huge hands the appearance of enormous fig leaves. Hence...

Every July, soon after my birthday, I put a dozen fig leaves in the oven. As birthday rituals go, it is calmer than eighteen-year-old me might've imagined. As with sowing chillies on Valentine's Day, the precision of the date isn't critical, but having a notable day to tie it to means it rarely gets overlooked. Over time, the day and the ritual become as interwoven as the branches on the fig tree itself.

The leaves go into the oven not to cook as such, but to dehydrate. It intensifies their flavour and extends their shelf life. Ten to twenty minutes at 130°C/110°C fan/260°F is all they need to curl into pistachio-coloured poppadoms, for the veins to turn to copper wire, and the house to fill with a gorgeous coming together of scents from my childhood: popcorn, malted milk biscuits, Shredded Wheat, coconut and candy floss. There is even a deeply pleasing hint of baby's scalp.

Infused in sugar syrup and dairy of all kinds, that biscuity flavour can light up cocktails, custards, rice pudding or make a fine ice cream.[2] Blitz a couple of the dried leaves in a coffee or spice grinder and the dust that results brings malty coconut pleasure to whatever it's sprinkled over: hot chocolate is a good place to start.

1 He was Northern Ireland's goalkeeper, one of those with the rare distinction of playing for both Tottenham and Arsenal, fierce north London rivals.
2 Undried, the leaves can be used to wrap fish, infuse rice and so on – but I'm not so fussed about them like that.

The dried leaves will keep for months in a sealed container, but their flavour is most intense during the first month.

If you don't have a fig tree, keep an eye out: you'd be surprised at how many overhang garden walls,[3] and are planted in public spaces.

Fig leaf syrup

This is one of my favourite syrups, great in cocktails, in a piña colada mojito,[4] poured over a cake, or just with sparkling water and a squeeze of lime.

MAKES ABOUT 750ML (1¼ PINTS)

500g (1lb 2oz) white sugar
500ml (18fl oz) boiling water
3 dried fig leaves

Place the sugar in a bowl and stir in the boiling water to dissolve the sugar. Allow to cool for a couple of minutes, then add the fig leaves and allow to infuse. Taste using a teaspoon, and when the strength is as you'd like it, remove the leaves and bottle the syrup.

In the fridge this will keep for a couple of months or so.

3 It is always wise to seek permission before handling someone else's bush.
4 Find a recipe for this in my book *Herb*.

Fig leaf and olive oil ice cream

This is an extraordinary ice cream, tasting of all the things the leaves smell of. While you can add all 8 dried leaves in the recipe below to the milks to infuse, adding half as ground leaves strengthens those flavours and brings a peculiar, but welcome, note of green tea. The olive oil brings silk to the texture and just a little green bitterness to offset the sweetness.

By all means use sugar, ideally soft brown sugar, instead of honey if you prefer.

MAKES ABOUT 800ML (1½ PINTS)

400ml (14fl oz) coconut milk
200ml (7fl oz) milk, of whatever kind suits you best
8 dried fig leaves
1 tbsp granulated sugar
5 egg yolks
150g (5oz) runny honey
5 tbsp olive oil

Warm the milks together with 4 of the fig leaves in a medium pan over a medium heat, stirring occasionally until it just comes to the boil. Reduce to a simmer.

Blitz the remaining 4 fig leaves, broken up, in a coffee or spice grinder with the granulated sugar until it is reduced to a green dust.

Whisk the yolks, honey and oil together until smooth.

Remove the fig leaves from the pan, then gradually whisk a little of the warm milk into the yolk mixture until half the milk has been added. Pour this back into the pan of milk, whisking constantly. Heat gently, whisking frequently, until it forms a slightly thicker custard – it won't turn to thick custard, just thicker than it started. Stir in the fig leaf sugar and allow to cool.

Churn in an ice-cream maker if you have one; if not, pour into a plastic tub and freeze, removing when half frozen to whizz in a blender, before returning to the plastic tub to freeze solid.

Bonnington Square, Red Duke of York potatoes, The London Eye and an extraordinary tortilla

A little over a quarter of a century ago, I lived in Bonnington Square, London. Built in the 1870s to house railway workers, a combination of wartime bombing and a council keen on redevelopment meant that this rectangle of Vauxhall was largely empty and earmarked for demolition a century later. In came squatters. A housing cooperative was formed, a vegetarian cafe,[1] a whole food shop and a club sprang up, and the bomb site in the middle of the square transformed into a flourishing garden. It is an extraordinary story of urban, community transformation.

I had no idea of this when I moved there: I'd just fallen out of the back of the van of a relationship, via the 'to let' pages of *Loot*, into a fairly small room in a fairly rough-around-the-edges flat in the corner of the square. I was not in a great way.

Every day I cycled to an office just to the east of Euston train station. As lovely as the people were, it was becoming increasingly obvious that I wasn't suited to someone else's hours, to someone else's idea of how I should spend my day, to someone else allocating my time. I didn't have the brain or way of thinking to suit. I hadn't yet realised that was okay, that there were upsides to being wired a little differently to many, and I hadn't yet come up with an alternative scenario for life.

The London Eye was being constructed at the time, the wheel itself horizontal as it was slowly meccanoed together. Over days and weeks it was pulled to the perpendicular, like a slo-mo of a bicycle having its wheel repaired and readied for the off. On its last day, I couldn't help thinking it wasn't quite vertical. Even now, it looks like it's at three minutes to twelve, rather than spot on noon.

The four-mile cycle left me exhausted, running as I was on few resources. I'd lock my bike at work and walk the minute to a Portuguese café, where every day I ordered the same: coffee and a wedge of tortilla. The tortilla, tight with onions and potato, its surface rippled the colour of onion skin, came warm, and wrapped in greaseproof paper. The smell couldn't have been more savoury and I couldn't have been more hungry.

On a good day, I managed to get to my desk to eat it; on others, I'd push as much of it as I could into my face before I left the café. Every mouthful put me back together enough

---

1 You turned up with cutlery and £6 and someone from the square would be cooking that evening.

to get through at least some of the day. Often, I'd head back to the café mid-morning; occasionally for lunch too. I ordered the same, always, because no matter how much I ate, nothing tasted as good and no amount of it diluted the pleasure.

A year later, I was out of London, planless, heading for a future I didn't know. While it's always good to run to, sometimes it's necessary to run from. I was wise enough to know it was the last time I should work for someone else.

For many years, I tried to recreate that lifesaving tortilla, and while I made some good ones, nothing quite scratched the itch, until eight years ago a friend – food writer and Spanish food specialist Rachel McCormack – made me hers. It was extraordinary.

In that way I rarely play my favourite albums for fear of diluting their magnificence with familiarity, I've never tried to make it her way since. Today, with the Red Duke of York potatoes more than ready to be lifted from their raised bed, the idea fell into my head.[2]

More than a quarter of a century may have passed since I ate that London tortilla, but let me tell you, if you brought me wedges of today's impersonation of it three times a day for the rest of my life, I would not be unhappy. In many ways, food writing is a pretence I keep up that I wouldn't rather be eating this on repeat.

Bonnington tortilla

As much as this will be the most delicious tortilla you eat, it is in no way effective as part of a calorie-controlled diet. The secret, as Rachel showed me, is not to fry the onions and potatoes, but to gently poach them – confiting, essentially – in olive oil. There should be no crispness, only silk. You will need half a litre or so of olive oil, of which perhaps 60 per cent will be returned to you at the end to fry eggs and so on down the line: it is the most excellent of oniony, savoury by-products. You don't need telling where the other 40 per cent goes.

The second secret is to season as you go, repeatedly.

When you flip the tortilla, don't be too startled if it looks a little rough; the shorter cooking time makes the second side – the one you show the world – a whole lot more photogenic than the first.

2 I recreated it from memory, so apologies to Rachel if I have missed anything crucial.

If you can resist the urge to eat this all in one sitting, it is very good cold.

SERVES 4, IN THEORY

500ml (18fl oz) olive oil
200g (7oz) onions, thinly sliced
600g (1lb 5oz) potatoes, peeled (optional) and very thinly sliced – I used a potato peeler
8 eggs
sea salt and freshly ground black pepper

Heat the olive oil in a good-sized frying pan – mine is a 25cm (10in) in diameter – over a low-medium heat. Carefully add the onions and potatoes to the pan – the oil will only come two-thirds of the way up the potatoes and onions, but as they soften it will cover them like the shore on an incoming tide. The oil should be at a gentle blip, like the reassuring heartbeat from the hospital monitor of a film hero.

Cook in the oil for about 15 minutes or so, using a spoon to turn the potatoes and onions occasionally. Season well as they cook. Once cooked – test with a knife's tip; they should be soft but not collapsing – turn off the heat. Use a slotted spoon or similar to lift the potatoes and onions out into a bowl.

Pour off all but a tablespoon or so of the oil from the pan into a heatproof bowl and return the pan to a low-medium heat.

Beat the eggs in a bowl. Pour half into the frying pan, then carefully spoon in the potatoes and onions. Season well. Add the rest of the eggs and use a spoon to spread the potatoes, onions and eggs until reasonably well mixed.

Cook for 7–8 minutes over a low-medium heat, running a spatula or dinner knife around the edge of the pan to round off the circumference and ensure it doesn't stick. Turn off the heat and place a plate that fits the pan well over the top. Using oven gloves, flip the pan upside down so that the tortilla turns on to the plate, cooked side up.

Place the pan back on the heat and slide the tortilla off the plate into the pan, using the knife and a little shaking of the pan to get it into place. Allow to cook, using the knife once again to round the edges and ensure it doesn't stick; it should only take 3–5 minutes to finish cooking. When ready, drain off any oil if you need to, then flip again on to the plate and serve with some crisp and plainly dressed lettuce, or tenderstem with a pinch of smoked paprika.

A huge lolly, Paul McCartney, sparklers and an outstanding baba ganoush

I have never seen a lolly like it. It is bigger than my hand and almost bigger than Dad's. It is purple and heart-shaped: I'm guessing blackcurrant. Wrapped in cellophane. He takes it from the top shelf. It has sat there for a month since I first saw it, holding me to attention, guiding my behaviour in case I am denied it for being naughty. For a month I have been good, or at least good enough.

He hands it to me.

'Wait till we reach the fireworks, eh.'

It is cold but the wind is light. There is a pile of wood and who-knows-what that has been building these last months. Gary walks past it on the way to school and has been keeping our class updated about it. The two miles between us and it mean climbing the big hill twice tonight. One day I'll come down it on the way home from school without brakes.

People stream out of side roads, everyone headed the same way. It's like I'm in the video for Mull of sodding Kintyre. I see Colin through the crowd and wave. He's got a hotdog too.

We are there in no time. I'm nervous. The bonfire and fireworks happens at what Gary tells me is the loony bin. I'm not sure if it's filled with loonies. Surely not: I can't imagine a lot of bangs and whizzes would do them any good. Mum pulls out what look like three paper rulers from her coat pocket. She hands my sister and I one each: a Curly Wurly! God I love a Curly Wurly.

She tears the top off the third: sparklers. This might be the best night ever. She hands one to each of us. Dad flicks the top on his lighter and we dip the four ends into the flame. Gasps as the ends catch. Our faces light up. Four smiles. We draw silver coils in the night. I write my name and my eyes almost remember the start as I get to the end. Dad says it smells like when a gun is fired; to me it smells like that time the car engine got too hot on the long way back from Lancashire.

A man with a loudhailer counts down from ten. By '7' all of us, half the town, are shouting along. A whoosh fills the air. The bonfire is alight. Everyone cheers. Even this far away, the heat finds my cheek. I can see the front of everyone and the back of no one.

My sister and I take the first long tugs on our Curly Wurlys. The toffee stretches, the chocolate cracks; eventually it breaks, leaving a long golden tail like a dragon's tongue. She chews like the cows beyond the churchyard, side to side as much as up and down, trying to keep her teeth from sticking together with the toffee. I realise I am too. We smile at each other.

A noise like a deep distant drum silences the crowd. A single bright dot draws a wavy line towards the moon. Up, up, up. Kaboom. Everyone gasps. It has started.

Up they go. Ting ting ting, three in a row, each splits with a crack into half a dozen stars, which impossibly spray into a series of falling cascades. It is like a Disney film and I am in it; we are in it. For I'm not sure how long, spiralling whistles and glitter fill the sky… bangs wider than the moon shake the town, shooting stars and UFOs skate across the sky. Joy crashes over me and soaks me to the bone. Nothing can beat this, nothing.

We are still flying when we leave; an excitement that takes us up the hill without realising. At the crest I resolve to freewheel down here soon: I will. Last week I had a dream that walking down this hill towards home I felt sleepy, so sleepy my lids closed and I had to prise them open with my fingers to make the last hundreds of yards to the house. Tonight my sleepiness is trumped by the magic.

Away from the flames, I can tell we all smell of warm smoke. The wind picks up. I plunge my hands into my coat pockets and there it is, the lolly I'd forgotten about.

Baba ganoush

You can turn a tight wedding day balloon of an aubergine into a slack honeymoon homecoming one by laying it on a tray and roasting it in the oven, but do it on a gas hob and the house fills with the scent and memory of bonfires past, even in August.

Smokiness is an ingredient, every bit as crucial as the lemon or the salt; if cooking aubergines on the hob isn't practical or you are an electric/induction lover, make the paprika in the recipe smoked to inject a little sense of the flames.

MAKES A BOWLFUL

1 very large aubergine (eggplant), or 2 medium, 450–500g (1lb) or so total
juice of 1 lemon
2 tbsp tahini
1 garlic clove, crushed
2 tbsp extra virgin olive oil
generous dusting of paprika
sea salt and freshly ground black pepper

Place the aubergine/s (one to a burner if using two) directly over a gas flame on the hob. Use tongs to turn occasionally until the skin is charred to the point of cinder and the flesh completely tender. Remove from the heat, cut with a knife and place cut side down in a colander to cool and release the juices.

Open the aubergine/s like a butterfly, scoop out the flesh and chop it with a knife. Worry not about a little charcoaled skin in the mix. Season with salt and pepper, and place in a good-sized bowl. Discard the skin.

Stir the lemon juice into the tahini to loosen it, then add the garlic and two-thirds of the oil. Mash this into the aubergine – you can whizz this with a stick blender but it becomes too smooth for my liking. Besides, the baba ganoush seems to know you took the care to use a fork, and rewards you in its flavour.

Season to taste, drizzle with the remaining olive oil, and dust with paprika. Serve with flatbreads, carrot batons and other crudités, or – if you are coarse and from Devon – spoon it on to a seemingly never-ending line of excellent toast.

Hummus

Because you really ought to have at least two dips on the go at once, for variety, here's my hummus. I almost always use pre-cooked chickpeas as I'm rarely planning ahead when I make it, and I almost always use the incredible jarred chickpeas that we know and love. This is really a taste-and-tweak recipe due to the variability of chickpeas, tahini, strength of garlic, juiciness of lemons etc.

MAKES A BOWLFUL

300g (10oz) cooked, drained chickpeas, plus a little reserved liquid
2 tbsp tahini
juice of 1 large lemon
1 garlic clove, grated
sea salt and freshly ground black pepper
generous sprinkling of freshly ground cumin

Whizz all but the cumin in a smallish bowl using a stick blender, adding as much of the chickpea liquid as you fancy, and taste for seasoning and lemon juice, adding more as needed. I've gone slightly smoother today than I might usually, just to contrast with the baba ganoush.

Dust with cumin and serve.

Mulberries, cabbage whites, Brian Setzer's quiff and a superb cranachan

I am sat on the sofa, bifolds open, *Day/Night* playing low, the dog occasionally slinking his trying-it-on way towards a corner around which I cannot see him, the weather shifting between overcast with a breezy hint of October, and glorious August sunshine. Right now, the lightest of glittery drizzles is falling. And as I reach the end of the word 'falling', the sun picks out the sparkle for a moment and the drizzle is gone. The wind seems to know when the rain stops, picking up again as the sun lights up everything.

A thistle has taken its chance, finding a gap in the sea of chocolate mint; the breeze lifts fluffy clocks from it – like the skeletons of bubbles – into the air, many holding hands in pairs.

Cabbage whites flap about as if being worked by amateur puppeteers – graceless yet beautiful – threatening to land here and there, but doing so only rarely, wings closed, in two dimensions. They do a loop or two of our garden, then off to a neighbour's before returning a few minutes later to repeat the circus. I'm not in the least fussed. You can lose years mithering yourself about potential nuisances to come and miss how beautiful they are right now, right here. The cabbage whites sniff the brassicas; if they stop, I rarely see them as they lay eggs on the underside of leaves to be more hidden from view. It's a nuisance, but I'm perfectly happy to check once in a while for caterpillars, as nothing shall come between me and my Nine Star broccoli.

The Pakistan mulberry is without fruit this year – a shame, as the berries are particularly long and juicy, the flavour exceptional – but the sight of its leaves are partial compensation,[1] shaped as they are like Morea (now the Peloponnese) in Greece where they also grow abundantly, hence mulberry's genus, *Morus*. Our white mulberry has a few fruit, and if the blackbirds have an appointment elsewhere, we get to enjoy them.

Thankfully, the young mulberry trees in the park are flourishing. The fruit ripen in waves – deep purple, dark red, orange red and yellowy green are all carried at once – which means you can pick the darkest knowing you have plenty more to come. I walked past them this morning and there were only so many that were deeply, lusciously

---

1 Maybe this summer I shall get around to stuffing some.

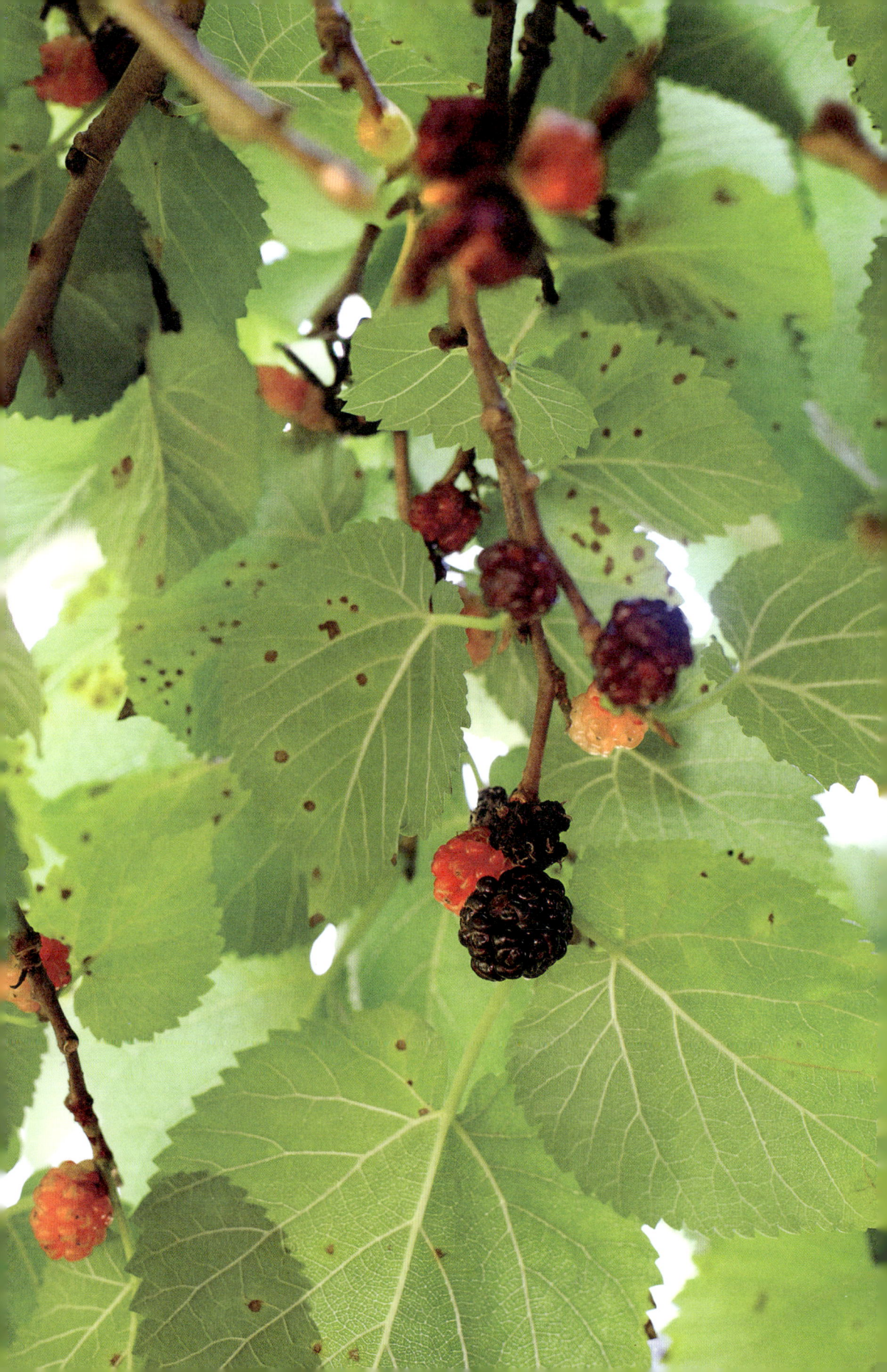

falling-apart-under-the-weight-of-their-own-juiciness, so I took a few on the red side of purple – they are wonderful in their slight sourness. I filled a spare dog poo bag with them, more than one passing walker doing a serious James Finlayson double take comparing the fullness of the poo bag with the hound they presumed responsible.

I can think of three sliding-door moments upon which my life turned at right angles. Without them, I might be sat at a bar boring myself and everyone in the postcode. I might've had the sense to make that bar in the far west of Ireland, but other than that life might well not have had much to recommend it.[2]

Eating my first mulberry around 2000 was most definitely one of those moments. It set off a tumble of decisions, luck and intuitions that led to our previous place, Otter Farm, to me writing, and being here today, in your company. If someone in a grey, airless office hadn't given me and the team I was leading the contract for the Suffolk Landscape Assessment, I wouldn't have been staying with a friend whose mulberry just happened to be in mid-August fruit, and that evening wouldn't have been blessed with the first taste of the finest fruit I've ever eaten, along with rather too much of the mulberry vodka made with the previous year's harvest. That evening I knew I had to find a patch of land to plant a few mulberries, and from there, the road led to here. Thank you Pat and Rob. I owe you.

Mulberry cranachan

I have never been to Scotland. I meant to walk the West Highland Way three times, and each time something sizeable got in the way – a job offer, a death and something else apparently not sizeable enough to stay in my Teflon mind. Despite that, I have a peculiar attachment to Scotland due to nothing more than Kenny Dalglish, shortbread, The Associates, Sean Connery and cranachan. One day I shall cross the border and experience its delights. Until then, I shall make do with playing 'Party Fears Two' while eating this.

This version is fairly full-on Scottish, with the pine nuts and oats, and even more so if you go for the smoky whisky and mugolio, or Scottish heather honey. I'd choose an Islay whisky for the smokiness it brings – Lagavulin if the book advance has recently come in, but Talisker or Laphroaig will do extremely well – but it is differently delicious without the whisky.

2 Buy me a pint of Guinness, ideally on the west coast of Ireland, and I'll tell you the story of the two of clubs (one of the other sliding-door moments).

SERVES 4

100g (3½oz) rolled oats
100g (3½oz) pine nuts
400ml (14fl oz) double (heavy) cream
8 tsp whisky (optional)
120g (4oz) mulberries[3]
4 tbsp honey or mugolio (see page 103)

Toast the oats and pine nuts in a dry frying pan over a medium heat, tossing to prevent burning, until lightly golden. Tip on to a plate and allow to cool.

Whisk the cream (and whisky, if using) until it forms soft Brian Setzer quiffs, stir in two-thirds of the oats, then spoon a little into four glasses. Follow with a few mulberries, a little more oaty cream, another layer of mulberries, more cream, the rest of the oats, and then drizzle with the honey or mugolio (if you are making this ahead, refrigerate and add the oat and honey topping just before serving).

Mulberry martini

I know some are disparaging of too much vermouth in a martini – perhaps humming 'Nessun Dorma' as they pour the gin, or just waving the glass in the direction of Puglia – but a good vermouth here acts like a gorgeous seasoning to the mulberries. Enjoy this in the garden, ideally while not watching your mulberries being eaten by the blackbirds.

SERVES 1

6 mulberries
80ml (3fl oz) gin
20ml (¾fl oz) dry white vermouth[4]
ice

Squish four of the mulberries in a cocktail shaker and skewer the other two on a cocktail stick. Pour the gin and vermouth into the cocktail shaker, add a handful of ice and shake for 30 seconds, then pour through a fine sieve into a chilled glass. Lie the mulberry cocktail stick across the rim, admire it for a second, then allow it to submerge, soaking in just a little booze to be a delicious treat.

3 A purée of gooseberries (with elderflower cordial in place of the honey) works so well here, as do blackberries at the end of summer.
4 Schofield's English Dry Vermouth, from Asterley Brothers, is very possibly my favourite.

Late summer fruit, Mr Windy, a flat cap and a great Sunday breakfast

On the way to the sea this morning I found myself behind an elderly man, flat cap on, hands locked behind his back, the largest of hearing aids bending his ears towards the perpendicular. As I got within a few yards it became apparent that he was farting at length and at great leisure, without a hint of either restraint or effort; a sound not unlike the last of the bath water emanating from his own plughole. He couldn't have looked any more content with his lot as we exchanged hellos while I overtook.

There's always some twit wanting to tell you it's autumn halfway through June, but these last mid-August mornings and evenings really have carried just a hint of chill. It lasts no time at all – by the time Mr Windy caught me up a few minutes later while I waited for the hound to finish his business, his hat was in his hands, behind his back – but the chill was there nonetheless.

Soon enough – maybe even in three weeks – thoughts will turn to the approaching cosiness and flames. And you know what, I'll be ready. I was made for May and September – wired for Nick Drake and John Martyn,[1] more *Murder Ballads* than 'Murder on the Dancefloor', a lover of the shoulders more than the body of summer – but even I'm not hurrying it along.

These cool bookends to the day, the old man's hat and his easy morning pleasure remind me to fully enjoy what's here while it's here; that now is for the best of the late summer fruit, yellow fennel flowers as some turn to lime green fennel seeds, the lemony zing of Buckler-leaved sorrel seed and other bright flavours.

This morning, while the house slept, I plucked mirabelles from the young tree, chose the plumpest, ripest blackberries growing by the greenhouse, grabbed handfuls of seed, flowers and leaves and made this rather special breakfast – a breakfast that somehow suits Sunday more than any other day.

---

1 Especially when the latter sings 'Solid Air', which he wrote about the former.

Late summer fruit panzanella

Panzanella is an Italian joy based around stale bread, onions and tomatoes, usually in combination with basil, olive oil and vinegar. This sweet variation takes the spirit of that classic and turns it to the best of late summer's fruit. The onions can do one, obvs.

It is hugely adaptable; swap in other stone fruit like peaches or add strawberries or raspberries as you fancy. This makes more cinnamon sugar than you need, but keep it in a sealed tub for a grateful future you. I used lemon juice to add a little sour bite, but I have a feeling red wine vinegar would be superb too.

Depending on which fruit you use and its degree of ripeness, you may find you want to tweak the flavours, so keep a little extra handy. Fennel flower's flavour varies with stage of development – the nearer to seed it is, the larger and more intense it becomes – so use half and leave the rest to hand for people to add if they wish. And if you have no fennel flowers, use fennel seed that's been bashed a little with a mortar and pestle, starting with 1 tablespoon and adding more if you think it needs it. Similarly, a little pinch of cinnamon sugar might be good for some.

SERVES 4

ok olive oil
4 slices of brioche
1 tbsp ground cinnamon
2 tbsp caster (superfine) sugar
10 mirabelles, halved and stoned
1 nectarine, stoned and cut into pieces
4 plums, stoned and quartered
16 blackberries
juice of 1 lemon
80ml (3fl oz) double (heavy) cream
a dozen basil leaves, thinly sliced
good handful of sorrel seeds, or use the grated zest of 1 lemon
4 fennel flower heads, torn into mini florets
good olive oil
sea salt and freshly ground black pepper

Over a medium heat, warm a good slick of the ok olive oil in a frying pan large enough to accommodate 2 slices of brioche. Lower the brioche in when the oil simmers and fry it for perhaps a minute: check often as the sweetness of the bread means it turns quickly.

Turn each piece over when lightly golden and season with salt and pepper. When golden on each side, remove to cool and drain on kitchen paper, and repeat with the other slices of brioche.

While the brioche fries, stir the cinnamon thoroughly into the sugar. Place the fruit into a large bowl and stir through the lemon juice.

Tear the brioche into pieces and sprinkle generously with perhaps a third of the cinnamon sugar, more if you have a sweet tooth.

Tumble the fruit and brioche together on a serving platter, drizzle with half the cream, shower with basil, the sorrel seeds and the fennel flowers, then zorro with the good olive oil, season with salt and pepper and serve with excellent coffee, and the rest of the cream in a jug in case needed. Eat in the garden, ideally.

Tomato leaves, baked bean juice, Joel Fleischman and a seriously good tomatoes on toast

Of the many impossibilities of life, as unfathomable to me as any, is that all the architecture of growth, the instruction of form and colour and flavour and scent can all be held in a single tiny tomato seed. In that tiny nugget – a 4B full stop – lies everything I see before me, including the scent that will cling to my fingers for the afternoon.

My senses never tire of the scent of tomato leaves. I might, *might*, just grow tomatoes for that smell even if they didn't fruit. It is one of the sweetest rewards – one of the great incentives – for growing some of what you eat. It occurs to me that the majority of people on this island have no idea what tomato leaves smell like. Why would they? It is up there with never having seen *Northern Exposure*, read *Hamnet* or eaten Honey & Co's incredible cheesecake for breakfast pudding.

If you are similarly deprived, the almost impossible task of orientating to the tomato leaf smell from other scents reads something like: bright, herbaceous and 'green' – there's something of the smell of fresh cut grass about it – with a hint of hay's muskiness, freshly cut hardwood, a touch of cucumber skin, the interior of green apple, and – perhaps most weirdly – baked bean juice.

I wondered if that tomato leaf scent might be captured for a little longer than on my fingers. I have a few side branches sat in a bottle of vodka, the logic being that perhaps a Bloody Mary of sorts or a heresy of a martini might result. I shall report back if it's good; you'll never hear of this again if not.[1]

Pesto is the elephant in the room. I would not be the only numpty to unimaginatively throw garlic, good oil, lemon juice, Parmesan and nuts at a green leaf in the hope of civilising it into something bearable. Carrot top pesto is the very definition of the crucial line between edible and delicious.[2]

So I took an incremental approach, making and tasting the pesto in stages. It led me to three very distinct, very delicious winners.

1 September me says it's very good.
2 Honestly, some things were made to be composted.

Let me say straight up, as flavoursome as the sauces are, the scent of the leaves doesn't quite translate wholly, but it is there like a favourite song leaking out of the small window of a neighbour's house, bringing pleasure. In the sauce it gives the impression of exaggerating the olive oil's flavour; in the pistou it makes the tomatoes taste even more of themselves; and in the pesto – against the blandness of pasta – you pick it up as if you'd scratched your nose four hours after rubbing the leaves.

Tomato leaf sauce, pistou and pesto

This is actually one process caught in three stages of development, each at its best in different scenarios.

The pistou is my favourite – I'm not as much of a fan of pesto as many – but you may prefer the others. This makes the sort of amount you might use over a few days or a week at most. The sauce is grassy and really good drizzled across fried eggs; the pistou is the five-ingredient sauce with Parmesan stirred through – it is perfect dotted on top of thick vegetable soup and here with tomatoes on toast; the tomato leaf pesto, the pistou with crushed pumpkin seeds added, is superb served unfussily with spaghetti.

FOR THE SAUCE

2 tbsp very good olive oil
generous pinches of sea salt
4 tomato branches, leaves only
1 garlic clove, chopped
1 tbsp lemon juice

Place half the oil, the salt and tomato leaves into a mortar and pound with a pestle until the leaves start to break down. Add the garlic and continue working it all into a smoothish paste. Add the lemon juice and the rest of the oil and incorporate thoroughly. Taste and add more salt if required.

FOR THE PISTOU

7g (¼oz) grated Parmesan
1 tbsp very good olive oil
squeeze of lemon juice

Stir the Parmesan thoroughly through the sauce, adding as much of the extra oil as you like to reach the consistency you want, followed by another squeeze of lemon juice to balance. Taste and season as you fancy.

FOR THE PESTO

handful of pumpkin seeds, chopped

Add the chopped pumpkin seeds to the mortar of pistou and crush with the pestle until the consistency is as you'd like it – I prefer the coarser side of smooth.

Tomatoes on toast with tomato leaf pistou

You really have to make this, even if with the best tomatoes you can buy rather than your own homegrown. The pistou makes the tomatoes taste more of themselves, and brings a gorgeous whiff of the leaves' scent – how something can taste of a smell I'm not sure, but it does nevertheless.

The herb flowers are optional, but if you have them in your garden don't be too lazy to pop out for them: oregano flowers along with the smallest of soft leaves add a lemony lightness, basil flowers bring a soft aniseed that tomatoes love so well, and if you are one of the few with winter savory, rejoice, for the touch of resinous diesel sings very happy harmonies with the olive oil.

As good eaten within an hour of getting up as it is before you go to bed.

SERVES 2

1 tbsp olive oil, plus a little extra to drizzle
400g (14oz) tomatoes, smaller ones halved, larger chunked
toast
1 tbsp tomato leaf pistou
oregano, basil or winter savory flowers (optional)
sea salt and freshly ground black pepper

Warm the oil in a frying pan until it shimmers. Add the tomatoes, stirring every half minute until the smallest think about collapsing and the larger pieces give in just a touch: 3 minutes max.

Spoon the tomatoes on to the toast, with just a very little of the juice.[3] Dot with the pistou, swizz with olive oil and sprinkle with salt, pepper and a few oregano, basil or savory flowers if you have them.

Bloody Mary

On the grounds you shouldn't drink a Bloody Mary on your own, certainly not early in the day, this recipe makes enough for two: all you need is an accomplice. If you are intending to consume both yourself, may I just confirm the health benefits of the tomato juice and lime are considerably outweighed by the incapacitating properties of the vodka. I've made this with tomato leaf vodka (page 177) and can report that a hint of the leaves' summer scent persists to very pleasing effect.

MAKES 2

celery salt
1 lime, halved
2 large handfuls of ice
500ml (18fl oz) tomato juice
100ml (3½fl oz) vodka
a slosh of Worcestershire sauce (optional)
a few shakes of Tabasco (optional)
freshly ground black pepper
2 celery sticks

Tip a thin layer of celery salt on to a plate. Squeeze the lime juice evenly between two tall glasses, then rub one of the halves around the rims. Dip the rims into the celery salt, then tip a handful of ice into each glass.

Split the tomato juice and vodka between the glasses, then (if using) slosh a little Worcestershire sauce and Tabasco into each. Stir with a teaspoon, taste and adjust. Place a squeezed lime half into each glass, sprinkle with a little black pepper and prod in a celery stick should you wish to be annoyed by it jabbing you as you drink.

---

3 Save the rest to drink with half as much vodka, a dash of lemon juice and a sprinkling of salt in the Bloody Maryest of chef's perks.

Squeaky beans, Deputy Dawg, a straw hat and two knockout summer recipes

I wish I suited a hat. At best, when placed on my head, a hat – of whatever kind – looks like a practical joke; at worst, something I'm doing for a very deserving charity. I'd like to look as gorgeous as Marlon in a hat, as cool as Clint, or like I had been born to wear it like David Rawlings;[1] instead I'm Deputy Dawg.

Nevertheless, I have dug out two: a woolly hat that my head will soon call for on early dog walks, and a straw hat I resolve to wear whenever I'm in the garden from St Valentine's Day.

I resolve to wear a hat because in a few days, a skilled lady will remove a small oval from my cheek in hope and expectation it is nothing tedious. That woman, a specialist in the organ that covers us,[2] tells me every time I see her that 'the skin remembers'.

Perhaps in those days when smoking was good for you, when no one spoke about their feelings (because we didn't have any, obvs), a me in small packaging was – as was fashionable at the time – packed off to frazzle, largely unsupervised, at the seaside for the day, merrily entertained by a football the weight of a balloon, a Dairylea and sand sandwich, a spiral of ice cream showered in hundreds and thousands, and a net made – it seemed – for efficiently lifting seaweed from rock pools while in search of crabs.

These were days of suntan lotion rather than sun protection cream,[3] the antidote to which was either top-of-the-milk (really) or calamine lotion. Even now, the scent of the latter tightens my skin to cheap greaseproof in memory of those evenings when so burnt I couldn't move my shoulders enough to get a shirt on. Pulling off jigsaw pieces of peeling skin was as much of a summer holiday pastime as anything back then.

Two of my closest gardening friends – neither as pasty as your correspondent – have similarly lost a small portion of their external real estate to the sharpest of blades. 'The skin remembers': I find myself repeating the words to my daughter. She will ignore them,

---

1 In a close race between Jimi Hendrix, Glen Campbell, Nick Drake and David Rawlings, it might just be the latter that I'd happily sell one of the two kidneys I have to play like. Or maybe I should choose Prince and then I could play like anyone.
2 Until our first meeting, I had no idea that the skin was an organ, our largest.
3 I had browner-skinned friends who routinely covered themselves in olive oil to sunbathe.

as is customary (and indeed, right and proper) when a parent offers unsolicited advice to a teenager.

I've chosen the 14th February as the first day of the year to become Deputy Dawg as this is the day I sow tomatoes, chillies, aubergines and other sun lovers, and while I will do this indoors, it marks the start of spring in my mind, of intentions towards the longer days, being more conscious of what's to come, and engaging with the growing year.

For the last few years, my wife has grown almost all of the annual vegetables[4] – those sown, grown, harvested and gone in a single year – and right now summer-into-autumn me is very grateful to late-winter her for sowing those tomatoes in the propagator. Next year, with her busy on the herb allotment she's developing, I'll be back on the seeds.

Every year I do it, I grow five varieties of tomato: three favourites and two that are new to me. It's a good rule for gardeners old and new. The law of averages means that even if you are beginner, three varieties will be special, one will be pretty good and one will be well… ordinary. Eat the three best ones, cook the pretty good one and give someone you pretend to like the ordinary ones. The two new varieties are important: they keep the door open to new flavours, to the possibility of new favourites, and frankly it's important to keep changing even the small things up.

There was a time when I couldn't imagine a better tasting cherry tomato than Gardener's Delight or Peacevine Cherry, but Honeycomb is genuinely such a wild upgrade on both that August-into-September wouldn't be August-into-September without them.

So when I light that first fire of autumn, when the needle drops softly on to 'River Man', after I've slipped a stack of personal admin – safer burnt than recycled – into those first flames as if guiding paper into a fax machine, I will make a seed list and tomatoes will be top of it. And while I can almost smell the first log fire of autumn, I'm going to try to remember to keep my hand on summer's end of the changing seasonal baton a little longer. There's still so much to pick and to enjoy.

And now I look at it in the hall mirror, that straw hat at least isn't entirely ruined by being placed on my head. And it looks a darn sight more fitting than the dressing I'll soon be sporting. So I will wear that hat from spring. I will be a good boy, and hope the skin remembers.

---

4 Costoluto Fiorentino, Honeycomb and Shimmer are the tomatoes I recommend to anyone who'll listen. Streamline, Polestar and Scarlet Emperor are my favourite runner beans.

Fresh tomato, runner bean and tarragon pasta

While I can take no credit for this year's tomatoes, the beans and so on, I can at least turn them into something that does them justice. This is the easiest, freshest, most wonderful of pasta dishes, and it uses raw tomatoes – retaining the brightness and delicacy of their summer flavour – alongside just-cooked and still-squeaky runner beans. It takes little time or effort – only the beans are cooked for the sauce – but you'll have to commit five minutes of your time the night before.

I've been making versions of this raw tomato sauce for 30-odd years – it is so light and fresh, with a serious garlic poke – and I'm particularly attached to this iteration, where the height of the green bean season meets the best of the greenhouse. This is differently splendid with basil, but I am deep in the arms of tarragon love at the moment, hence it is in both of these recipes, though it is very swappable if you prefer. Parmesan might be to your liking – I prefer it cleaner, without – but on you go if you fancy.

SERVES 4

700g (1½lb) large, ripe tomatoes
6 garlic cloves, finely chopped
2 tbsp red wine vinegar
10 tbsp olive oil
50g (2oz) tarragon, leaves only, roughly chopped
300g (11b 2oz) pasta – something like fusilloni that will cling on to the sauce
400g (14oz) runner beans, stalks removed
zest of 1 lemon
sea salt and freshly ground black pepper

Half-fill a large bowl or pan with boiling water and lower the tomatoes in. After a couple of minutes, lift the tomatoes out of the water. Cut a cross in the end of each and remove the skin. Chop the flesh roughly, discarding the tough core. Place in a large bowl with the garlic, red wine vinegar, olive oil and tarragon. Cover and leave in the fridge overnight.

The next day, bring a large pan of salted water to the boil and cook the pasta according to the packet instructions. Drain.

Meanwhile, bring a medium pan of salted water to the boil and lower the runner beans in. Return to a simmer and cook for anything from 2–5 minutes depending on their size and

variety. They should be firm but giving to the bite, and still squeaky on the teeth. Drain and refresh with cold water to prevent the green turning to khaki. Slice on the angle, into 5cm (2in) pieces.

Stir half of the tomato sauce into the pasta. Add the beans to the rest of the sauce and then stir this into the pasta. Season generously and spoon into four bowls. Sprinkle with lemon zest and serve immediately.

Cherry chana chaaty salad

Chana chaat is a classic Indian street food classically bringing together chickpeas, tomatoes and cucumber with the sour spiciness of chaat masala spice blend. The observant of you will notice an absence not only of one of the key ingredients but also the spice mix that lends its name to the recipe. I can only apologise. I did at least add a 'y' to the recipe title. What replaces those missing elements is the sweet pleasure of a good handful of cherries and a combination of extra lemon and smoked paprika. The usual coriander is switched for tarragon. Authenticity is not something that this recipe might be accused of. It is, however, delicious (I promise).

It would be completely usual to serve chana chaat splashed with plain yoghurt, dashed with pomegranate seeds and fresh chillies, and showered in sev or Bombay mix; I'm sure that would work well here, but wanted something simpler today. Embellish as you wish.

SERVES 4

250g (9oz) cooked, drained chickpeas
16 cherries, torn open and stoned
1 red onion, very thinly sliced
3 ripe, good-sized tomatoes, finely chopped
small bunch of tarragon, leaves only, roughly chopped
juice of ½–1 lemon
1 tsp smoked paprika
1 tsp hot paprika
sea salt and freshly ground black pepper

Stir the chickpeas, cherries, onion, tomatoes, tarragon and half the lemon juice in a large bowl, then season to taste with salt and pepper. Add more lemon juice if a little more zing is needed, sprinkle with both paprikas, then serve with crisp lettuce and good olive oil.

Tomatoes, happy heartbreak, Bowie and tomato and rosemary soup

Everything is still. There will be no 'Paper Machete' cutting through the morning, no 'Dreams' filling the air ahead of a cloud of perfume following her down the stairs and out to wherever.

The first day of nursery, it hit me that we are always letting them go, in mostly invisible increments, and I imagined today. No one writes songs about your child flying the nest but they should.[1] It is perfectly brilliant and entirely awful. I couldn't be more happily heartbroken.

We return to an empty house and all I can think is that there is no point cooking; that I can't imagine just us being worth the effort of cooking again. In a wave like hangover guilts, I resent every single moment of these last 18 years, 10 months and 26 days that I have been elsewhere. In the rain, I fold away her sun lounger into the garage and wonder how my autumnal self will get by without her daily summer.

We get up and walk, despite the rain. We walk up the hill, through woods, out on to the cliff where the view is almost too short to see the sea in the rain and mist. One of us stops to cry invisible tears.

Along the seafront we stop for coffee and yoghurt-frosted flapjack like it's 1998. The sea is completely in and almost completely still, like grey/green linen. The lack of swish on the stones, never mind crash on the rocks, is eerie: it reminds me of that first football match, on the terraces at Turf Moor – 10 years old and colder than I've ever been – taking 15 minutes to realise that the unsettling feeling is the lack of commentary I'd become so used to from the telly. I hadn't realised there are no replays.

We follow the river towards its source and talk about everything and nothing. The last of the Costoluto Fiorentino tomatoes need picking, my wife says, maybe I'll make soup. Somehow I make the soup: I think she knows what I don't, that something slow to do is exactly what I need.

---

1 Other than in unhappy circumstances, like 'She's Leaving Home' by the Beatles.

She picks the tomatoes that she's cared for all year; I turn the oven on. A random prickly wave rises, the air is too much in my chest, my eyelids too heavy, the kitchen top takes my weight and everything stops for a minute. And then it carries on. As luck would have it, there are just the right number of tomatoes for the roasting tray.

A text: *It is all amazing.* Everything lifts.

This morning, the sun is out, house martins draw erratic lines across the sky ahead of their migration.

In three weeks, five weeks, two months or three days she will be back with her appetite and trail of detritus. Clothes will once again litter the floor as if shot out of the sky. There will be a new rhythm, a new season. It might take a day or two to get used to the absence of her constant sunshine, to not pick her up a takeaway brownie from the café we love most, but it's time – as Bowie sang – to turn and face the strange. It is all absolutely as it should be, and there is soup for lunch.

Tomato and rosemary soup

If ever two people made a soup, this is it, and if ever a soup sang loud of the end of summer, here it is. Not only does it taste so completely of the essence of tomatoes – like childhood sickbed Heinz Cream of Tomato Soup (with its tomato soup moustache) does in your memory rather than how it does in reality – it is also the easiest, with everything cooked in the oven. I used ginger rosemary, but regular rosemary will be excellent too.

For something more of a main course, warm the soup with a few spoonfuls of butter beans or white beans, add croutons, and Parmesan is most definitely your friend here.

MAKES 2 LITRES (3½ PINTS) – ENOUGH FOR 6–8

2 leeks
1.8kg (4lb) largish tomatoes
4 garlic cloves, cut into the same number of slices as there are tomatoes
20cm (8in) rosemary, leaves shredded from the stem
olive oil
double (heavy) cream
basil leaves, thinly shredded
sea salt and freshly ground black pepper

Preheat the oven to 190°C/170°C fan/375°F. Wrap the leeks in foil and place them in the top of the oven.

Core the tomatoes with a short-bladed knife, using the thumb of your knife hand to prevent you cutting (the tomatoes or yourself) too deeply. Place them in a roasting tray, push in a sliver of garlic, a clutch of rosemary leaves and half fill each core hole with olive oil. Sprinkle with salt and pepper and place in the middle of the oven.

Check the tomatoes after 30 minutes or so: you want them softened but not collapsing, and before the skin has blackened. Allow to cool a little. Remove and discard the rosemary leaves.

Check the leeks – they are done when they take a sharp blade with no resistance: they may need longer depending on their size. Tip the leeks into a colander and allow cold water to run over them until just cool enough to handle. Strip off the outer layer and the base.

Blend a leek plus however much of the tomatoes your blender can comfortably take on high until smooth, repeating in batches until all is blended. Taste and season well.

Pour into a pan and bring slowly to a hint of a simmer, then ladle into bowls, swirl with a little double cream and olive oil and sprinkle with basil.

A glossy purple clot, Tom Waits, brown betty crumble and two excellent drinks

No matter how many years I take to the hedgerows, my heart overrules what my head knows: blackberries are a late summer fruit. Seamus Heaney knew. 'Summer's blood' is in them.[1]

And yet it makes no sense: blackberries – complex and indirect – taste of autumn, with none of strawberries' easy summer brightness. Strawberries are 'There She Goes', an easy-to-love open book; blackberries are all 'The Heart of Saturday Night' and feel like they have something left to tell you.

In the days when an entire Saturday was given over to the FA Cup Final, blackberrying caused families – kids grumpy at being torn from the telly, parents bickering after a fruitless search for Tupperware lids to match their tubs – to stream from homes as if called by an invisible church bell.[2] Out to verges, overgrown hedges, and – in our case – the semi-choked path of the old railway line, in search of free fruit.[3] What Beeching discarded, nature reclaimed.

For every blackberry we popped purple-fingered into a tub, we ate two. It was not without jeopardy: Heaney's weren't the only hands 'peppered with thorn pricks', and there was the last of the Jasper Luftwaffe[4] and the seed-heavy nettles to contend with. As delicious as those blackberries straight from the bush were, Mum's blackberry and apple pie – to see us through the weekend before going back to school – was the real prize. These decades later, I can still taste it.

I do pick a few blackberries in August, hoping for 'heavy rain and sun for a full week', but I don't enjoy it the same as when I have a cold nose,[5] though this means playing stick or twist with early autumn sun ripening those that are 'hard as a knot' in mid-August.

---

1 Even the most poetry-averse cannot avoid falling for Seamus Heaney's paragraphs of perfection in 'Blackberry-Picking'.
2 See also: Bonfire Night's firework display, the carnival, Concorde passing overhead.
3 If you are British, it is incumbent on you to pass this peculiar pastime on to your children, along with reticence, irrational unfocused shame and an inability to express your feelings.
4 Is it only in Devon that we call wasps by this name?
5 Having a later blackberry season is, along with dandelion and burdock and musical brilliance, one of the more compelling reasons for living in the north.

Out on this morning's footpaths winding up towards the woods, among the honeysuckle and beech, there are still plenty of blackberries, if marble-small and tight. I grow some in the garden too, and this sunny week has seen a late flush. While the peak of homegrown blackberries may come earlier, larger, juicier, sweeter and more heavily than their wild relatives, I certainly wouldn't choose them over the complexity and the gentle palaver of foraging.

Folklore has it that Archangel Michael defeated Satan in battle, banishing him from heaven to hell, arse-first into a blackberry bush, causing him to spit on the bush and curse its fruit – hence you oughtn't to eat blackberries after Old Michaelmas Day (10th October), but good luck finding some so late, or – if you do – free of mould.

I think the plant in the garden might be Oregon Thornless, or possibly Waldo: whichever, a sunny afternoon this month with the football on the radio will find me dealing with the old stems. Each year, blackberries grow long shoots (canes) that develop fruiting side shoots (laterals) the following year; my job is to tie the young canes to the arch to fruit next year and prune the old canes with their spent laterals back to the base (they'll not fruit again).

It's one of those gentle interventions that connects you to the garden, simultaneously to the moment and to next summer – or should that be autumn? So much of what goes on out here is popping something in the bank for another time, that future-you will be grateful of.

Apple and blackberry brown betty crumble

Many years ago, I came across a recipe for brown betty – imagine a layered dessert of, alternately, stewed apple and sweet, spiced breadcrumbs – and it sounded too good to be true. It almost was. This takes the best of it and combines it with the never-unwelcome crumble topping.

You could, if you prefer, have two fruit layers with the apple and blackberries mixed, but like this, the blackberries soak into the breadcrumb layer and just hint at spicing the apples.

SERVES 6

90g (3¼oz) bread, crusts removed
30g (1oz) butter, melted
50g (2oz) soft light brown sugar, plus extra if needed
5 largish eating apples
juice of 1 lemon
300g (10oz) blackberries

FOR THE CRUMBLE

80g (3oz) plain (all-purpose) flour
40g (1½oz) golden granulated sugar
80g (3oz) butter, cut into cubes
40g (1½oz) rolled oats
good pinch of sea salt
nutmeg

First make the crumble by whizzing the flour, sugar and butter together in a food processor. Stir through the oats and salt, then tip the crumble into a large bowl.

For the breadcrumb layer, whizz the bread in a food processor until it forms largish crumbs. Add the butter and sugar and whizz in short pulses until it forms medium breadcrumbs – don't worry if you over-process it and it starts to come together a little too much, you can always tease it into more of a crumb.

Preheat the oven to 210°C/190°C fan/410°F.

Peel and core the apples, cutting them into smallish chunks; as you go, place them in a bowl and stir through the lemon juice to prevent discolouring.

Place the apples in a medium baking dish, 20 x 20cm (8 x 8in) or so. Add just enough water to coat the base to encourage the apples to give in, and stir with a little extra sugar if you like your crumble on the sweet side. Spread the breadcrumbs over the top. Dot with the blackberries. Spoon over a thin layer of the crumble mix and then add a very generous scratching of nutmeg. Spoon over the rest of the crumble mix.

Place in the centre of the oven and bake for 30 minutes. Use a cake skewer to see if the apples have surrendered to the heat; if not, cover with foil to prevent the crumble burning, and give it a little longer. Once you are happy with the apples, remove the foil and allow a few minutes for the crumble to finish cooking if needed.

Remove from the oven and leave to rest for 15 minutes to allow the crumble to develop crunch and the fruit to calm down from being molten lava.

Serve with custard, or cream, either soured or double.

Blackberry whisky

This is an extraordinary drink, peculiar in that – had you not known its constituents – you are unlikely to identify either the blackberry or whisky in the result. It really is so very good, and while you may – as I would've been before tasting it – be hesitant to risk a bottle of smoky single malt, you will be well rewarded. That said, a bottle of blended will make you a very, very fine version too.

Put 600g (1lb 5oz) of blackberries and 700ml (1¼ pints) of whisky into a jar large enough to accommodate them both. I used to add 120g (4oz) caster sugar but I no longer do: it just doesn't improve for its addition. I favour an Islay single malt – Laphroaig or similar – as its smokiness works so well and adds a little more autumn to the result. Seal the jar and upend and shake whenever you remember to over the next couple of months. Strain and funnel into a sterilised bottle and allow the flavour to develop: a year is good, longer even better, but I know you've seen Christmas around the corner and I won't deny you a tot or two.

Don't discard the boozy fruit, it is wonderful with stewed apples or added to a crumble.

Honeyed blackberry vinegar

Blackberry vinegar is – depending on your disposition – either a superb, vaguely balsamic-like vinegar that suits beetroot, goat's cheese and anywhere a fruity/sharp dressing might be required, or a superb, effective cold remedy. I have to say, on those nights where you have a little hankering for a glass of what you fancy, this with three parts sparkling water[6] and a slice of lime works wonders.

The weight of sugar or honey varies a little: it should be three-quarters the weight of the strained vinegar, e.g. if you have 500g (1lb 2oz) vinegar once strained, add 375g (13oz) sugar or honey.

300g (10oz) blackberries
500ml (18fl oz) apple cider vinegar
caster (superfine) sugar or honey

Place the blackberries in a good-sized jar and add the vinegar. Allow to infuse for 14 days or so at room temperature.

Strain through a sieve, catching the liquid in a pan. Bring to a gentle simmer. Stir in the sugar or honey until dissolved, then boil for 5 minutes.

Funnel into warm sterilised bottles and seal.

6 Yes, or sparkling wine…

Professor Yaffle, the log pile, Cary Grant and a sunny day salad with a very special dressing

The clank of early morning copper pipes is my autumn alarm clock. I was made for these days: 6°C when I wake and in the early 20s by lunch. A late morning of open windows and doors while making stew for the evening, my thoughts turning to the log pile in late afternoon, tells you a very great deal about both the season and me.

Today, my wife and I left early, eyes streaming, into the cold still light. A loop with the hound of perhaps an hour and a half, give or take a lean on a gate.

Woodpeckers might be my favourite bird, though don't tell the kingfishers. They look homemade to me, their wings set back a little too far, their heads a touch large, their feathers as if coloured in by a seven-year-old. They fly in soft dips and lifts, like a brilliantly made paper aeroplane, with no fuss or over-embellishment. We stopped to stare at the photoshop contrast of vivid blue sky and the lime green of autumn's leaves, and a woodpecker – not one of the pair we'd just watched darting across the fields – started up right above our heads. Every 15 seconds, its beak working on a fat trunk, sounding like a fairytale door.[1] Why this always lifts my heart, I don't know. Maybe it's talking to the infant me watching Woody Woodpecker repeats; more likely *Bagpuss* with Professor Yaffle, the woodpecker bookend.

The birds seem to enjoy these days as much as I do. The air above the fields is busy with house martins and swallows swooping low as if dusting crops where there ain't no crops, searching for the many insects you find where cows and their piles of dung ferment in the autumn sun. Between them, they make one of the more compelling arguments for livestock.

Swallows – their long, dark, forked and strongly pointed tails, pale undersides and dark heads – are typically farmland birds, nesting in outbuildings and taking advantage of the plentiful food supply; house martins – appearing completely pale from below, with a short, forked tail not unlike a mackerel's fins – are typically found around towns, making mud nests in the eaves of houses. They'll both soon line up on telephone wires like notes on a stave, ready to fly to warmer winters. The woodpeckers, thank heavens, are staying here to keep me company.

---

1 Some days they sound like a ruler being twanged on the edge of a school desk.

Fig, watercress and burrata salad with honey and fennel dressing

I may be making stew for the evening, but lunch belongs to the sun, just. The last of the figs and only a few weeks of watercress to come, makes this an early autumn special I couldn't love more.

The fennel seeds – by all means use your own green seeds if you have some growing – is the secret thread sewing the figs and burrata even closer than they might be. The parsley can be left as whole, with just the coarser stems snipped off, and woven in with the watercress, or, as here, roughly chopped.[2]

SERVES 4

1 tbsp runny honey
2 tbsp red wine vinegar
2 tsp fennel seeds, lightly bashed
4 tbsp good olive oil
100g (3½oz) watercress, well washed
6–8 small, ripe, jammy figs, quartered
300g (10oz) burrata, drained
quick pickled onions (opposite)
40g (1½oz) pine nuts or hazelnuts, lightly toasted
small bunch of flat-leaf parsley, roughly chopped
sea salt and freshly ground black pepper

Add the honey and vinegar to a small jar, along with a generous pinch of salt and the fennel seeds, then seal and shake the jar vigorously. Add the olive oil and shake once more.

Scatter the watercress over a platter and dot with half of the figs. Tear the burrata into sloppy threads and blobs and dot across the platter. Add the rest of the figs – this is because it looks better to not have too many hidden from the hungry view of those about to eat. Sprinkle as much of the onions as you like – half the quantity here may be enough, depending on your preference. Scatter with the pine nuts, sprinkle with parsley and splash generously with half of the dressing – leave the rest for people to add to their plate if they wish. Season generously and serve.

2 The larger pieces mean that not every mouthful has parsley, but when it does it's there with impact.

Quick pickled onions

If you can be arsed enough to make this once, you will make it often – it really is as special as it is simple. Get these onions in burgers, sandwiches, tacos, or sprinkled through and across salads where you want a little gentle acidity and muffled onioniness. This works beautifully with red onions – they turn a luminous pink.

2 tbsp sea salt
1 red onion, very thinly sliced
juice of 1 lemon (or 2 limes, or ½ orange)

Rub the salt into the onion slices between your hands; the same action you might make to keep your hands warm. Lay them on a plate for the salt to draw out the moisture and soften the onions. Rinse the onions in a sieve. Return the slices to the bowl, add the citrus juice and leave to stand for about 30 minutes, though it will be pretty good after 10 if you are in a rush.

Grapefruit and elderflower dressing

I make versions of this with all kinds of citrus, and it's this version I like best as an alternative to the honey and fennel dressing if – as is often the case – I'm eating this frequently in late summer.

2 tbsp grapefruit juice
4 tbsp elderflower cordial
1 tbsp French mustard
2 tbsp extra virgin olive oil
sea salt and freshly ground white pepper (black will do)

Whisk the juice, cordial, mustard, a good pinch of salt and a generous peppering together in a glass. Add the oil, whisking to create an emulsion. Taste and add a little more salt and pepper if needed.

Crabby rooks, Steve Martin, three-pint lunchtime and the best baked potatoes

Southeast Cornwall in autumn: the sky is dotted with screeching buzzards and scratchy rooks, while below, a seascape of alternately calm wide blue and simmering grey-green claws at the land. It's been a week where the weather gave a little of everything: it rained heavily, sunned intensely, blew impressively. We took the best for walking; the worst for reading, drinking excellent coffee, visiting a subtropical garden (grateful for its natural overhead protection),[1] and eating the best of pasties.[2]

Much of it was spent with my wife like Father Ted and me like Dougal, with her trying to bang into my thick head the difference between a crow, a rook and a jackdaw. We didn't even get to ravens.

In much the same way I still have to imagine a compass to remember which is west and east, I turn to the old rhyme – a crow in a crowd is a rook, a rook on its own is a crow – and I know jackdaws are the smallest, but by the time I've remembered the rhyme,[3] whatever the feathered thing was has moved on.

There are other corvid identifiers – a crow is all black with a dark eye, a rook has a lighter, grey face, a jackdaw has a pale eye and neck, and so on – which all serve to heighten the sense that I am extremely dim for not more easily telling them apart: the case for the defence extends only to 'when you are looking through glasses misted by drizzle and a steaming flat white, it can be hard to tell your arse from your elbow'.

I do know that should you happen to stop mid-walk beneath them to tie a shoelace, rooks will make a hellish noise to hurry you along your way.

The hedges stole the week. Many carry the last knockings of blackberries (so full of juice and flavour), some are thick with tight rose hips, and there's the occasional sweet waft of honeysuckle. A hedge of American elderflower at the fabulous Potager Garden near Constantine was out-marvelled only by the trimmed hedge of Chilean guava, abundant

---

1 Trebah Garden.
2 From Gear Farm Pasty Co – Karen Barnes (kbjoyousthings.substack.com) put me on to them and she was, as usual, most correct.
3 Or I've confused myself with a variant… ('a crow on its own is a rook…').

with fruit: when I wrote about these fourteen years ago in *A Taste of the Unexpected*,[4] you could find them almost nowhere.

Now and again, out on the path or in a village, the sun lifted the scent from a stretch of ivy, reaching my nose a good half minute before I saw the flowers. So heady and dense is the perfume, it felt like a three-pint lunchtime. If you didn't have asthma before, it feels like it could bring it on. The entire postcode population of bees made their way to it.

Elsewhere, the stoniest of seemingly uninhabitable walls provide enough shelter – where a glint of sun shines through the canopy – for a few hardy things to set down roots; there was an unexpected meeting with a huge maritime pine and its astonishing bark; the frequent, if localised coupling of fuchsia and old man's beard; another smaller pine with limpet shell rings hung on its fingers; wild chamomile and rock samphire in glorious profusion along the Coverack coast; chicory dotting a field here and there; huge gunnera striding towards you like giant spiders.

The Helford Estuary has magic. At the risk of sounding like Navin Johnson, Steve Martin's character in *The Jerk*, a weekend here feels like a week, and a week a fortnight. To list the ingredients, identify the elements and snap little vignettes is like talking about the first chord of 'A Hard Day's Night' – really interesting – but the magic of the chord[5] and of the Helford is in the invisible lace that weaves it all together.

Twice-baked potatoes with rosemary creamed leeks and smoked paprika

I'm not especially interested in spending too long in the kitchen chopping and peeling when on holiday in the colder months. Assembling, throwing in the oven, having this or that on toast when not eating out is very much more my holiday style. It's the same for at least a week when I get back. And this fits the bill perfectly.

4 Yes, since you ask, that is the book for which I first won Food Book of the Year, but I'm too modest to mention it.
5 One of the things that makes me happiest is unnecessary brilliance. No one would've thought anything unusual had 'A Hard Day's Night' begun, as anyone else in the world would have, after that first chord. That it's there is genius enough, but McCartney's D and Harrison's added low G and C are beyond glorious.

SERVES 4

4 baking potatoes
2 large leeks, tough greens trimmed
2 garlic cloves, peeled
200ml (7fl oz) double (heavy) cream
20cm (8in) sprig of rosemary, leaves only, finely chopped
1 tsp smoked paprika
sea salt and freshly ground black pepper

Preheat the oven to 210°C/190°C fan/410°F.

Place the potatoes on a baking tray and into the oven for about 1 hour, until cooked and the skins are crisp.

Meanwhile, cut the leeks lengthways from the green end to about a third of the way along their length, and wash thoroughly. Place a clove of garlic in each cut, wrap in foil, and place in the oven at the same time as the potatoes. After 30 minutes, check to see if the leeks are done – they should happily take the point of a sharp knife without resistance – if not, allow them a little longer until done. Unwrap the foil and allow to cool a little while the potatoes continue to cook.

When cool enough to handle, remove the garlic from both leeks and squish to a purée. Peel the toughest outer layer off the leeks, slice off the root ends and discard both. Chop the leeks on the fine side of roughly and place in a bowl, seasoning well.

Add the cream, garlic purée and rosemary to a small pan and slowly bring to the boil. Boil for a minute or so until just hinting at thickening, then remove from the heat.

Cut the potatoes in half and scoop out the flesh, leaving the skin plus a little extra as a boat into which you will sail the filling back into the oven. Mash the potato into the leeks, along with three-quarters of the cream. Season well. Carefully scoop the mixture back into the potato halves, place back on the baking tray and cook for 10 minutes or so until colouring nicely.

When ready, pour over the rest of the garlic rosemary cream and sprinkle with the smoked paprika. Crisp, quartered little gems dressed in excellent olive oil are very good on the side.

Japanese pepper, Paul Newman, living to 99 and pan haggerty

It has been raining all day. Proper rain. Rain that has you daydreaming of an early evening bath, of potatoes in combination with cheese, of a hoppy ale by a fire inefficiently burning with the door open, the flames better to see.

We escaped the house mid-afternoon, disbelieving of the forecast that it would ease off, but needing air, a slice of the world – specifically, steaming coffee and a chocolate cookie, sat in a shelter on the cliff, the seat wiped dryish with napkins, watching the sea chat with the clouds, while the water that fell on the land ran away back to the start of the cycle, to fall again another day.

I have been feeling old. Old for pasts unpursued; pasts lost to time. This is ok. I know that every year around now, two things happen: a day or two of melancholy at the passing of the seasons and the years, always followed by the uplift.

There is so much I want to write, so many books I have proposals sketched for or even fully coloured in. I wish I'd found writing aged 20 or even 30; that I'd managed to overcome hesitancy at anything I wanted to do earlier than I did, but here we are: at least I found it and found the resolve to jump in, when so many don't or can't. Musical stardom, professional table-tennising and transforming this lanky frame into something resembling *Cat on a Hot Tin Roof* Paul Newman may be beyond me, but not much else. And on the upswing, I still believe those three impossibles might happen.

I had planned to clear the greenhouse of its ageing tomato plants, to harvest the good and compost the spent, to clear a path for winter and new beginnings. The beam of sunshine I apparently needed didn't materialise. Perhaps tomorrow. Instead, back from coffee and cookies, I made shichimi togarashi.

The Japanese sansho pepper is ripening beautifully in the garden. While the leaves are the classic harvest from this plant in Japan, the peppercorns are equally delicious. With rain forecast on my mind, yesterday I snipped off a clutch of them: the comparative warmth of the house caused the shells to open, revealing the seeds. These black globes are flavourless – it's all in the colourful casing – and this makes separating the two easy. A day makes all the difference.

I quite like rain, if I'm honest. And I've grown to value these melancholy days because they are the ones that make me live better. They are a reminder in the busyness of life. Bukowski's wild horses running away over the hills. Shaun Ryder, with a different kind of eloquence: 'You may be 20 now but you'll wake up next week and you'll be fucking 52, mate, so go and enjoy it. It's that fucking quick.'

In my book *Sour*, I wrote: 'I resolve to make it to 99. I'm already at the point in life where few things thrill more than a cancelled arrangement, so dodging a 100th birthday party should bring a special, final glee – and the prospect of another half century leaves me with no excuse not to fill it with the pleasure of [*insert your own desire*].' Shifting my goalposts to 99 means that I have a little more adult life left than I've chewed through. So, it's all ok. And if I don't make 99, whatever time I have will be better lived.

So while the cliffs may be wearing the clouds around their shoulders today, it will lift soon enough, and the view will seem even better for having seen today's. As John Lennon sang, 'When it rains and shines, it's just a state of mind'.[1]

Shichimi togarashi

This is Yuki Gomi's recipe, which she kindly let me use for my book *Spice*. This classic Japanese seven-spice is superb in many Japanese recipes, but I'm very much the off-roader with it – I love it on chips and roasted vegetables, aubergines especially.

MAKES 20G (¾OZ)

2 tsp dried satsuma skin[2] or yuzu peel powder
1 tsp hemp seeds
2 tsp ichimi togarashi or dried red chilli
1 tsp black sesame seeds
1 tsp roasted white sesame seeds
1 tsp aonori[3]
½ tsp sansho pepper

Dry the satsuma peel in the oven for 30–40 minutes at 95°C/75°C fan/200°F, then grind it into a fine powder. Grind the hemp seeds and the dried chilli into a powder. Mix everything together.

1 In so doing, inventing The Stone Roses a couple of decades before they formed.
2 The skin from a single satsuma will normally make around 2–3 teaspoons of dried powder.
3 A dried seaweed, is available online and in some supermarkets.

Pan haggerty

This old Northumberland classic is not to be confused with Den Hegarty, once a member of '70s band Darts, or Dan Haggerty, the actor who played Grizzly Adams in the series of the same name. You can make this on the stovetop, as is traditional, but why do that when you can slip it into the oven and not have to worry about it sticking to the bottom of the pan. This is somewhere between a dauphinoise (with no cream) and a Jansson's temptation (without the anchovies) and if ever a recipe suited a rainy but not especially cold day, where the cloud obscures the neighbour's chimney, this is it.

SERVES 4–6

2 tbsp olive oil
4 large onions, thinly sliced
1 tbsp caraway seeds
24 sage leaves, finely chopped
600g (1lb 5oz) potatoes (about 3 medium), peeled and thinly sliced
500g (1lb 2oz) sweet potato (about 3 medium), peeled and thinly sliced
500ml (18fl oz) chicken stock
200g (7oz) Cheddar, grated
2 tsp shichimi togarashi[4]
sea salt and freshly ground black pepper

Preheat the oven to 210°C/190°C fan/410°F.

Warm the olive oil in a wide frying pan (ideally with an ovenproof handle) over a medium heat. Add the onions, caraway, sage and a good pinch of salt, reduce the heat a little, and fry until the onions are soft, stirring often. Remove the onions from the pan.

Arrange half the potatoes in a layer in the bottom of the pan, followed by a layer of half the sweet potato, seasoning with salt and pepper as you go. Spoon in all of the onions, then add the rest of the sweet potato, followed by the remaining potatoes, seasoning each layer.

Carefully pour in the stock, cover (with foil if the pan doesn't have a lid) and cook in the centre of the oven for 40 minutes. Switch the oven to grill (broiler) mode, remove the lid/foil, add the cheese, and grill until golden and bubbling. Sprinkle over the shichimi togarashi and serve with a squeaky green vegetable such as broccoli or tenderstem.

4 If you don't have shichimi togarashi or fancy a different mood, use 1 teaspoon of chipotle chilli flakes or smoked paprika instead.

Siberian chives, a slipped disc, oregano flowers, and focaccia

The dog has a slipped disc. Don't ask. Three times a day, I carry him outside to the patch of garden he thinks is his. After a fortnight, he's capable of doing the shortest of 3-metre circuits on level ground before he stops, staring straight ahead. It is the sign I should lift and bring him back in the house, where he resumes mithering anyone who'll listen in hope of feeding his addiction to the pills he's taking, or more likely the cheese in which they're disguised.

If the few owls that love our road so well, who call to each other from either end, are joined by one sitting in the ginkgo that overhangs our garden, Harris – reminded of the presence of an outside – will realise he needs a late-night pee. Open the door and he will sniff the air, sneeze twice at the change of temperature, and once carefully set down on four paws, pretend he is going to the camellia that grows by the window that, while no one particularly loves, thrives merrily enough that it seems unfair to curtail its exuberance.

The bed he likes best is full of unusual alliums, globe artichokes, *Tulbaghia* and other edible pleasures, and having pee-free ingredients is – I think – the very minimum my family – and readers – expect of me.

The dog is fooling no one. He knows that he's allowed to wander among the plants as long as he doesn't entertain the idea of a pee until he's off that bed and nearer the compost bins. Having pretended he's interested in the camellia, he sneaks to his favourite bed. He almost always stops by the Siberian chives, looks over his right shoulder, and checks I see him about to pee: 'On you go', I tell him, and he does as he's told.

This late at night, my mind isn't wandering; it's not distracted by anything to get back to. I notice three young globe artichokes growing on a single plant. Every year I forget that autumn brings a second spring-like rush of growth. The crisp summer stem and gone-over flowers on the globe artichokes are being pushed into the background by glaucous new growth. I could pick a few of these new artichokes, but my heart's not in it; other than an early summer vignarola (page 121), I mostly want artichokes just boiled into submission, to pull to pieces, each petal dipped in hollandaise, a dry white wine and summer sunshine to accompany. Whatever pleasures autumn may offer, it's not the time for artichokes; they can stay as they are for whatever creatures climb the stems in search of overwintering.

As the hound makes his way back his side brushes against the Siberian chives; a couple of flowerheads rattle. The driest are full of seed, about to fall; the greenest hold tight to the immature seed within.

This morning, I'm back with the secateurs. A dozen or so of these rattling flowerheads rubbed against a palm release enough seed for a small jar; some to sow for more plants, the rest for the kitchen. The tiny black seeds are similar to nigella seeds – with perhaps a touch more bite – and I use them for oniony punctuation in salads, on potatoes, with eggs, and – where I like them best – in bread.

A few steps behind the Siberian chives in its life cycle, the oregano is in flower. The cold that most years would've been here to darken the tender flowers has yet to arrive; for once, the snip of the kitchen scissors will beat that of the frost. The flavour and scent of oregano flowers is close to that of the leaves, though there's maybe a touch less diesel about them; a gap between the first semi-acrid hit and the smoothness of what follows. If you have leaves – dried even – they work differently well in the recipe below. And if the cold is coming and you're in a rush, snip the flowers off and whizz them with salt in a food processor or using a stick blender: depending on how dry the flowers are you'll end up with a paste of some kind – a coarse adjika of sorts – that you can sprinkle wherever you think salt and oregano might work. A midweek jacket potato is very glad of its attention.

Onion seed and oregano flower focaccia

This is the easiest thing to make. Just let the dough rise rather than pay too much attention to exact timings, as they'll vary depending on the temperature of your house.

This recipe is highly adaptable: try 50/50 bread flour and '00' pasta flour; swap the olives for cooked shallots, gooseberries etc.; and in place of oregano flowers try sage, rosemary or any other woody herbs that take your fancy.

This will make either one 25cm (10in) square focaccia or two smaller ones. Don't worry if your tray is larger than this: the dough doesn't have to fill the space.

One big tip when making focaccia: soak any herbs you're using in a little oil – just enough to coat them – as without that, the herbs will desiccate and lose much of their intensity to the heat of the oven.

MAKES 1 LARGE OR 2 SMALL LOAVES

350ml (12fl oz) warm water
10g (¼oz) active dry yeast
generous handful of oregano flowers, or oregano/other woody herb
180ml (6fl oz) extra virgin olive oil, plus extra to serve
500g (1lb 2oz) bread flour
flaky sea salt
3–5 tbsp onion seeds, to taste
70g (2½oz) olives

Stir the water and yeast together and let it sit for 5 minutes until foamy.

Chop the oregano flowers and sprinkle a little of the olive oil over them.

Add the flour, 1 teaspoon salt and 4 tablespoons of the olive oil to the yeasty water and mix well for about 10 minutes, either by hand or using the dough hook on a mixer. Add half the oregano flowers and half the onion seeds towards the end.

Tip into a large bowl brushed with olive oil, cover and let it rise in a warm place until it doubles in size – about 60–90 minutes depending on the temperature and other apparent randomness.

Brush your baking tray(s) with a little oil. Tip the dough on to the tray and use your fingertips to flatten it, then brush the top with oil, cover and leave for 20 minutes.

Dip your fingers in oil and press and stretch the dough into a large rectangle, leaving the dimples from your fingers. Press the rest of the oregano flowers into the dough, followed by the olives into the same dimples, and sprinkle with the rest of the onion seeds. Cover and allow to rise for about 40 minutes. Meanwhile, preheat the oven to 220°C/200°C fan/425°F.

Brush the top with a little oil and scatter with flaky sea salt. Bake in the centre of the oven for 20–25 minutes until golden. Once out of the oven, drizzle with oil, sprinkle with salt, and feed again with yet more oil; now try and allow it to cool and soak in the oil for at least 10 minutes before diving in.

Figs, fennel, a dozen willies, and an autumnal crumble

The only thing that's not *really* moving in this wind is the fennel. It seems to know where to cast its seed from one year to the next, so as to inhabit the most sheltered spots. This year, one grows close to the stem of a sansho pepper whose spiky branches pin it in place; there's another growing in a crack in the concrete by the back wall; and this one by the greenhouse, where the fingers of these chilly autumnal winds can't quite get a grip on it.

Perhaps in the way we now know a field of mushrooms is likely just one subterranean organism waving dozens of willies in the air for us to pick, we'll one day discover the same is true of fennel. However many spring up – and there are three more on the other side of the house – all are welcome. The seed – held at the fingertips of the outstretched hands that were its flowers – are small, numerous and full of a sweet aniseed that brightens the mouth and mood. Get them green and they are bright as toothpaste; as they brown and dry, the flavour softens just a notch, developing a peculiar delay where their flavour releases a few seconds after you chew on them, much like the pain of a stubbed toe.

Seeds from the shops are similar enough, but missing a little top end, as if the treble has been dialled down on the hi-fi. They're still pretty good, thank heavens, because I use way more fennel seed than I could hope to grow. Crumbles, shortbread, sausages, stews, cocktails and more.

The handfuls I pick at this time of year don't make a dent, but they do bring pleasure.

A few made it into a small precious batch of Chinese five spice – that wonderfully aromatic blend that so suits the sweet-sour cooking of its home region of Guangdong in southern China. Do try making your own, even just once, as it is so full of oomph, and if you grow your own pepper too, it takes it up yet another notch. Whizz this lot up in a coffee or spice grinder until nearer dust than rubble.

MAKES A SMALL JAR

2 star anise
2 tsp fennel seeds
10cm (4in) cassia or cinnamon stick
2 tsp Szechuan pepper
8 cloves

The rest of those just-picked seeds went into a crumble. I do like a crumble. Figs may not be a common fruit for a crumble, but they most certainly should be.

My daughter is ambivalent about figs. I think that for her they never live up to their purpleness: where is the implied blackberry, mulberry, blueberriness? For much of my life, I felt the same. There was one in Santorini when I was 22 that was so good I'm not sure I didn't dream it. Then a decade ago, a white fig – heavy as a cricket ball, a mint-coloured ripple across its flesh, juice dipping through my fingers, a drink more than a fruit – from an allotment off a roundabout in Tottenham, north London.[1] I saw the light.

While I wait on the two plants we bought last year to become productive,[2] and while I lack the daytime nerve to scrump the ones on a very public corner of a local park, I make do with early autumn figs from the greengrocer that seem to get better every year. Perhaps everyone in the chain is holding their nerve, waiting for that tear of nectar to appear at the eye of the fruit before they're picked. The couple of dozen I've had so far this season have leaked more than a little of their sweet syrup, and I've had to take particular care not to tear the skin when washing them. Their flavour is really something: close to really good, plump raisins in honey and sherry.

Strictly speaking, figs aren't fruit. Tear one open with intrusive thumbs, as if opening a book in the middle – and take a proper look: inside, a gazillion tiny flowers that somehow, in the absence of light, bloom and set seeds in secret. Sink your teeth into that luscious flesh and you're sucking on a sweet soup of yesterday's flowers. I love that.

Torn to ragged pieces, these flower graveyards make a fine salad with burrata and punchy leaves (page 206), but that's for late summer; autumn – and if I'm to get them past my daughter – needs a warmer, sweeter way.

---

1 I put Joe Swift on to it, and he took the *Gardeners' World* cameras to take a look into Chris Achilleos' incredible allotment.
2 The question I am asked most about growing figs, is about how to deal with the fruit that haven't ripened by the change of season. It's pleasingly simple. Figs may produce new figs twice a year – once in spring, once in summer, hence plants might have fruit of different sizes by summer's end: large ripening figs, tiny pea-sized fruit and smaller, and those in between. The large ones will soon by ready to eat, the small ones will develop into next year's fruit, and the ones in between should be removed in November as they'll weaken the plant without ever maturing.

Fig and fennel crumble

Figs and spices are very good friends. You could do far worse than try a good pinch of five spice in slashed figs before roasting, or a generous scratching of nutmeg, but here I've used fennel in the crumble mix.

Using olive oil rather than butter in a crumble is almost always the way I go these days; it makes life easy for vegan friends (and readers) and, equally importantly, the grassy bitter undertone works so very well with most fruit. This makes twice the amount of crumble topping you need but any less and the blender won't bite on the ingredients: freeze the rest for next time – for there will be a next time. If the figs are less than spectacular, a splash of sherry before you add the honey works well.

SERVES 6

110g (4oz) rolled oats
50g (2oz) caster (superfine) sugar
60ml (2¼fl oz) olive oil
2 tbsp fennel seeds
8 plump, ripe figs, tough stems removed[3]
good drizzle of honey

Preheat the oven to 210°C/190°C fan/410°F.

Whizz 100g (3½oz) of the oats and the sugar together in a blender, to form a rough flour. With the blender running, drizzle the olive oil in: when the mixing becomes ineffective, switch the blender off. Add the remaining oats and the fennel seeds and stir together with a knife to create the crumble.

Slice a cross 60 per cent into each fig, opening out the centre: each fig should look like the origami fortune-teller game you must have played at school. Place them in a tightish dish. They will now look like a clutch of starling chicks screeching for food. Into each of their gaping mouths, drizzle honey and use a teaspoon to tease in crumble so that it domes and overflows a touch: any that falls between the fruit will soak up the juices, creating a delicious fudgy, dunked-shortbreadiness at the base.

Bake for about 25 minutes until the figs are still just holding their shape. Serve with whatever form of yoghurt or sour cream takes your fancy.

---

3 The white milk that exudes is latex, a defence to keep predators at bay; it's harmless, perhaps even beneficial in its antibacterial properties.

Squash, rugby union, Baker Street and spiced squash curd

The summer-long conversation between the garden's contours and the plant's genetics placed a single Uchiki Kuri squash – the plumpest of the crop – on the garden wall. It must have reached that spot just as it had enough about it to drop anchor, for the plant to grow on without dragging the young fruit with it.

It is – of course – this one I'll use first.

Despite a malevolent army of an absent summer, incompetence and every mollusc in the southwest moving to this postcode, there are 21 good-sized squash in the garden; 21 squash present a challenge.

There are a number of things I feel bad for not liking more than I do – including Bob Dylan,[1] rugby union, sponge cake[2] – and squash is most certainly one. It's not that I don't love it, but I find squash the 'Baker Street' of vegetables: extremely welcome once in a while, especially if it appears unexpectedly. And having 21 is the very opposite of unexpected. Two things prevent those 21 from sitting on the side in the kitchen rotting and making me feel guilty for not using them in time: preparing them for a long life after harvesting, and having a few delicious recipes that buy you time to eat them. More of that in a moment.

Now autumn has stopped playing at it, the squash are ready to harvest. You can leave them a little past when the leaves surrender to the chill, but when you rap the fruit with a knuckle or dessertspoon and it rings hollow as a funfair coconut, it's time. Here in the rainy southwest, if the wettest weather comes early, I slide a slate under each plump fruit to keep them from sitting in the damp and rotting before they're ready to pick. This year, that wall saved me one tile at least. Whatever the weather, I pick and bring them undercover before the frosts hit – we cut them from the plant, leaving a short T stalk on each squash, as fewer rot that way and they seem to store longer. If I have to pick early, I flip them so their undersides face skywards while they mature. Right now, the 21 are lined up like pub-league trophies in the greenhouse, curing.

---

1 Much as I love Dylan's five classic albums, if you left my mum in a darkened room with a comb and tracing paper for sixty-one years, I suspect she'd come up with five cracking albums, without the very great deal of some of the worst throwaway pub blues ever created.
2 I never want to eat sponge cake again.

This is what buys you kitchen time. Leave squash for a week or two, ideally somewhere cool and dry, and much of their water evaporates, the flavour concentrates and sweetens, the skin hardens, respiration slows and shelf life extends. Just as City and United may be related, squash and pumpkins are very much not the same. Botany reveals little about the distinction between the closely related pumpkins, squash and gourds, but experience tells us much: squash have been bred and their seeds saved for generations with flavour uppermost in mind, gourds tend to be decorative and largely inedible, and pumpkins – with a very few exceptions – are generally orange, large, of no great culinary pleasure and most definitely best hollowed and lit with a candle.

Preparing a squash is like tackling a large, irregular baseball. I don't bother peeling unless I really have to, and I've learned the hard way that cutting into a wobbling squash is the quickest route to discovering that no one can remember the location of the first aid kit.[3]

First, I cut an inch or so off one end: this allows me to flip the squash on to a wobble-free base to cut in half through the poles (rather than the equator). A sturdy spoon and much enthusiasm is needed to scoop around the edge of the core and remove the seeds[4] and their associated threads of tedium. Placed cut side down, it's less hard work to slice each half into long, eye-shaped wedges.

Three recipes from one squash

For these recipes, one good-sized Uchiki Kuri squash provided enough flesh. I cut one half into four wedges, using three for the curd; I cut the other half into five thinner wedges, using them and the remaining thicker slice from the other half for the harira soup.

Place the wedges flesh upwards in a roasting tray and drizzle with a little oil – more is just a waste as it'll slip off and just fry the skin beneath. You can spice and herb it as you wish – salt, pepper, chilli, rosemary, cinnamon, etc. – but I almost always roast without, so that I can lean the flesh one way or the other once cooked. As here. Thirty minutes or so, at 200°C/180°C fan/400°F should do, but let the tip of a sharp knife sinking with luscious ease into the flesh tell you exactly when.

---

3 A selection of ill-matching plasters, mid sizes absent.

4 There's little point in saving the seeds to sow next year – squash cross-pollinate readily, so any seeds will give unpredictable results – and besides, they're delicious. Wash and dry them, lay them out on a roasting tray with plenty of sea salt and roast at 200°C/180°C fan/400°F for a few minutes to intensify their flavour.

Squash harira soup

Harira soup is a classic North African soup, heavy with sweet spices and tomatoes. While it is by nature highly adaptable – lentils, no lentils, *which* lentils? – I've stretched this a fair way from its origins on account of the wind blowing strongly today: warmth and comfort are needed; heartiness and heft essential. You could argue that it's more of a stew than a soup, and I'd not put up much of a fight: whether it becomes one or the other is yours to choose, depending on the amount of pasta and water you go for. The wind made me tip the pasta in to make it more of a supper than lunch: by all means drop the quantity or entirety of pasta if you wish.

I used red lentil pasta as one of those it is for eats no gluten. Orzo or noodles (around 100g/3½oz) work really well instead. Bear in mind the quantity of water here is a guide: the type of tomatoes and lentils will affect how much you need, and the texture is yours to choose. I prefer this on the thicker side of thin; you might not.

SERVES 6

2 tbsp olive oil
2 leeks, thinly sliced
2 tsp ground ginger
2 tsp ground coriander
10cm (4in) cinnamon stick
1 tsp ground turmeric
3 tbsp concentrated tomato purée (paste)
2 x 400g (14oz) cans chopped tomatoes
1.5 litres (2½ pints) water
200g (7oz) puy (French) lentils, well rinsed
160g (5½oz) pasta
6 wedges of cooked squash
sea salt and freshly ground black pepper

TO SERVE

plain yoghurt, if you fancy
harissa
olive oil
good handful of coriander (cilantro), roughly chopped

Warm the oil in a large, heavy-based pan over a low-medium heat and cook the leeks slowly until soft, stirring often. Season generously.

Add the spices and cook for a minute. Stir in the tomato purée, the chopped tomatoes and 1 litre (1¾ pints) of the water. Bring to a simmer and add the lentils, turning the heat to low. Cook for 30 minutes or so, stirring occasionally, adding more water if needed. Season.

In a separate pan, cook the pasta in simmering water according to the packet instructions. Stir into the soupy stew.

Place a wedge of squash into each bowl and spoon over the soup. Add a little yoghurt if you want, a teaspoon of harissa (more if you fancy the heat) and a drizzle of oil, then sprinkle with coriander.

Squash curd

Most people will tell you to make curd in a heatproof bowl over a pan of simmering water, but I do it in a pan over a low heat as my hob is responsive and I'm confident in making it. Either way, whisk frequently, bordering on constantly.

Butter is the usual source of silkiness in curd, but Thane Prince suggested cream worked even more beautifully and, having tried it, I can't go back.

The spices are yours to tweak: mixed spice gives a gorgeous, wide warmth and you can just add more if you prefer, but I like to lift with star anise and mace as they go so well with squash.

Try this with excellent bread or scones, in a tart, on porridge (honestly), stirred through whipped double cream and meringue on a very special autumnal Eton Mess, or – perhaps my favourite way – in an autumnal cranachan.

MAKES ABOUT 900ML (1½ PINTS)

400g (14oz) roasted squash flesh, skin discarded
1 star anise, ground
2 lanterns of mace
1 tbsp mixed spice
140ml (4¾fl oz) double (heavy) cream
270g (9oz) caster (superfine) sugar
2 eggs, plus 2 yolks

Add all but the eggs to a pan and use a stick blender to blend until smooth. Warm through over a low-medium heat, stirring frequently with a whisk.

Add the eggs and yolks one at a time, whisking each in thoroughly. Cook for about 10 minutes or so, whisking often and scraping down the sides if needed. Depending on the nature of the squash, you may need a splash or two of water if this gets a little too thick. If you have a kitchen thermometer, remove the bowl from the heat when it reaches 78°C (170°F); otherwise just ensure it is well cooked and hot.

Pour into a warm sterilised jar/s and seal immediately. This will keep for at least a month unopened, and for months in the fridge even once opened.

Squash cranachan

A classic Scottish pud that is as simple as cream, fruit, oats, honey and optional whisky, in ratios that please. The curd may have firmed up a little in the fridge; let it down with water or a glug or two of single malt if you fancy.

As a guide, use 100ml (3½fl oz) double cream whipped until it holds peaks softer than Walter Brown, then layer this in glasses or bowls with a few spoons of squash curd. Add a handful of rolled oats scattered on top and a friendly drizzle of honey to finish. Simple and magnificent.

There is another, more detailed, recipe for cranachan on page 171, should you wish to try it.

Borlotti beans, rain, a spider and a Muppet

The spider that's made its home between the handle and the corner of the Velux window in my office has no idea how lucky he is. What must be a month of forgetting to sweep the hoover's nozzle upwards has given him a web that – judging by his size – has done for many of the last of summer's flies.

In its cosy, happy existence, he has no idea that just a couple of centimetres away a fortnight of almost constant, big-drop cartoon rain has thrown itself towards him; a sandwich of glass separating him from a theme park ride down three floors of drainpipe and gutter to the garden drain. By now, I'd have expected to unblock that drain, but only the leaves that fall as the days shorten – rather than when the cold hits – have left the trees.

It's a peculiar autumn.

The cold comes only with the wind; the soil is as warm as the sea and what I usually might rush to pick ahead of mid-October cold is as happy as early September. The yacon has even thrown out a couple of new flowers this week, when I'd usually expect its beautifully soft leaves to be blackened by the cold.

And while this lack of chill means the lemon verbena and scented geraniums are safe for now, the mooli patch can grow on for a bit, the apios doesn't need lifting in a hurry, the woodland artichokes are – I hope – flourishing underground, I can feel all of that harvesting and processing ruckling up like waiting-room carpet, to be concertinaed into a few days who-knows-when as the cold finally hits.

For now, it rains.

And in the absence of any sign that it will end, the borlottis need my attention.

Along with salsify, borlottis were the first thing my wife and I planted that we'd never tasted before. The sunny autumn that followed showed me how much lay beyond the shops, how many incredible flavours there were to enjoy if you find a little time to grow them. While borlottis are now commonly found tinned – and pretty good they are too – a year without those glorious pods in the garden doesn't feel quite complete. Borlotti pods' shape is as unremarkably familiar as many beans, but their glorious splatter of crimson and cream is enough to render them spectacular.

The beans are loyal to the pods' colour scheme, although their crimson splashes seem in inverse proportion to the pod they're in, as if there's only so much paint to go round. You might think it doesn't really matter as the beans lose their mottle when cooked, but that bit of Jack and the Beanstalk magic still thrills whatever's left of six-year-old me.

I used to pick most of the borlottis in the heart of summer, while they were still soft, to make into hummus or ribollita, but I tend to leave them until September now, when the bean teepees look as shabby as Sweetums from the Muppets. At that point, the beans themselves are demi-sec – half dry – which means they're perfectly timed for the end-of-tomato-harvest soups.

For a collection of reasons, this year they remained unpicked into October. At some point, as their leaves fell and a few of the vines turned brown, it made better sense to let them dry out completely before harvesting. Ideally, the pods dry to witch's fingers on the plant; this year the rain has other ideas. They may be mottled Caramac and leather, but dry they aren't.

In one of those sunny intermissions that makes you wonder if it really was torrential an hour ago, we strip the plants bare, leaving the roots in the soil to enrich the ground with the nitrogen they've captured from the air as they grew. Brown and crisp as the pods mostly are, they're laid out on a table for the radiator to do its occasional work when the house drops enough for the thermostat to talk to it.

Every day or so, I'll split one lengthways to release the beans to see if they're ready. One of the things I love about leaving the beans this late is that the inside of the pod shines like an oyster shell. So many small pleasures.

Once a bean is so hard a cat couldn't scratch it, it is fully dry and can be stored in a jar to use anytime.

Borlotti's spiritual homeland is the Veneto region of Italy – Verona, Venice and Valpolicella – and its classic radicchio and borlotti soup and a cold-weather version of Tuscany's ribollita are exactly what I'll end up using these borlottis for. Maybe I'll try some in Boston baked beans.

And there it is again, the ping ping ping of fat raindrops on glass. The spider twitches in his web. Time to bring the washing in. Maybe next week, I'll put some borlottis on to soak.

Devon spiced beans

Back in the days of being unemployed and spending most hours of most days talking rubbish and listening to music (quiet at the back there...), it was not unusual to have curried baked beans on toast as the main meal of the day. This is my homage to that unpleasantness – a sort of vegetarian Boston baked beans that's neither from Boston nor baked. Use dried borlottis, homegrown or otherwise (soak overnight, rinse and simmer for 30 minutes or so), or canned as below.

SERVES 4 ON TOAST

1 large onion, finely chopped
2 tbsp olive oil, plus extra to drizzle
3 garlic cloves, finely chopped
½ tsp ground cloves
1 lantern or 3 strands of mace, or a very generous scratching of nutmeg
1 tbsp yellow mustard seeds
1 bay leaf
a few sprigs of thyme
1 x 400g (14oz) can chopped tomatoes
about 7 sloshes of Worcestershire sauce
½ tsp chipotle chilli flakes
2 tsp chipotle paste
1 x 400g (14oz) can borlotti beans, drained
2½ tbsp maple syrup
juice of ½ lemon
chopped coriander, to serve
Parmesan (optional), to serve
sea salt and freshly ground black pepper

In a large pan, fry the onion in the olive oil over a medium heat until soft and translucent. Stir in the garlic, clove, mace and mustard seeds and cook for 1 minute. Add the bay, thyme and tomatoes and simmer for 5 minutes or so. Slosh with Worcestershire sauce, stir in the chipotle flakes and paste, and season well. Simmer for another 10 minutes or so, adding a splash of water if it gets too thick. Add the beans and simmer for 5 minutes.

From this point, it's all about tasting and tweaking: stir in the maple syrup, season more if needed, and add as much of the lemon juice as you need to brighten the whole.

Eat in front of a lively blaze, on toast, swizzed with a little olive oil, sprinkled with coriander and a generous snowfall of Parmesan.

Medlars, Barbra Streisand, Airfix and two sheriff's badges

It's the first morning that the air – rather than the wind – bites cold. The sky is the blue I'd paint the underside of the old man's Airfix planes when he trusted me to; the sea – lapping softer than it has for a fortnight – straight out of *The Way We Were*.

The three-mile morning walk I do takes 42 minutes when I've a mind to get a bead on; today it's calmer and differently good with my wife for company. The medlar tree, planted a year ago, sits just to the side of the garden path and for the last few weeks its changing leaves have caught the eye every time I've passed it. Each looks like a miniature river basin seen from above: yellow river, green shallows, yellow inlets and orange-brown floodplain.

Today, as we get back, we check the fruit: half are firm, half soft, a few already fallen. Too young to produce enough for two harvests – the softer ones first, leaving the others to develop a while – the choice is leave them and lose some of the ripest to the slugs beneath, or pick the lot and figure out how to use them later. We chose the latter, persuaded as much by the pleasure of being unexpectedly in sunlight. We fill our coat pockets quickly, our hands too: the definition of not a lot but plenty.

Two decades ago, we moved to the middle of the land between Dartmoor and Exmoor, to two-and-a-bit acres of dampish ground, where we threw weekends and evenings into growing food. We had little idea. We grew too much of some and too little of others, but – it turns out – the food is only part of the point. An old second-hand book had us planting a medlar – a forgotten fruit, supposedly similar in flavour to cooked apple and dates. We left that place before it could fruit.

We moved an hour towards the coast: somewhere the wind didn't start blowing on 1st April and stop on 31st March. That winter, along with a very great deal of other things, I planted an orchard of medlars – perhaps forty trees – with a single one left over. I planted it on a long, stony island between the river and a ditch, where the sun would hit its leaves for every minute of every day. I'd see it as I approached and left the polytunnel, as I crossed the bridge into the far field, and as I span the tractor – mowing up and down the pecan and persimmon orchard – I'd catch sight of it and how it was developing. Alone, it showed off its medlar qualities even more clearly – a lazy irregularity of branches and a trunk growing with little respect for trees' vertical norms. This single tree became the barometer for the medlar orchard a few hundred yards away: it served notice, when its fruit was ready, that we had a few days – a week, perhaps – until those in the far field would need harvesting too.

When I picked medlars with my young daughter, it was from that lone tree. One small tree, one small harvest, nothing overwhelming like a whole orchard. When we were done, she felt like a grown-up, and little did she know those were the moments of my week.

We left the farm a few years ago now[1] and while I'm okay with that – you have to live looking forwards more than back – there are a few little things that bob to the surface now and again, and that medlar island is one.

Last year, in the front garden of the house we've been in for three years – where we might see it from many windows, where we would pass it leaving and returning to the house, under whose shade herbs and artichokes might grow – we planted a medlar. Today, it filled our pockets and hands with 1,106g of fruit, an amount that has little power to inspire guilt. Whatever the weather, however busy you may be, you can find a delicious use for 1,106g of fruit.

Medlar sticky toffee pudding may be the reason I was sent to this planet, and a couple of 200g (7oz) packs of medlar purée in the freezer mean I already have the necessary for this wintry essential. So this year, something different.

Six or seven years ago at the farm, I set about making membrillo – essentially, a posh Spanish fruit pastille made with quince – but an early arrival meant I had to cut it short. I jarred it anyway, hoping it would make an okay jam. I tried it next morning – a glorious carnelian lava somewhere between syrup and jam, that over the following months found its way into dressings, on to porridge and rice puddings, stirred through Eton Mess, fizzed up in cocktails, spooned over pancakes and more. Without a proper name, it became Quince Thing. Today, I made Medlar Thing. It turns out to be the best thing I've made when the quantity of firm medlars outweighs the soft, though it would work differently well with the ratio reversed.

The first mouthful drew out those memories like a stream of roped tyres falling over the side of a boat. And that – it turns out – is what growing and cooking so often does.[2]

---

1 I still have the plant and seed nursery, located not at the farm.
2 Jane Steward of Eastgate Larder has written a really special book about medlars – *Medlars: Growing & Cooking* – with some superb recipes.

Medlar thing

MAKES AROUND 1 LITRE (1¾ PINTS)

1kg – or 1,106g (2lb 4oz) – medlars, some bletted, most firm
2 sheriff's badges of star anise, broken up
500g (1lb 2oz) caster (superfine) sugar
juice of 1 lemon
a small knob of butter
2 tsp ground ginger

Wash the fruit and chop into quarters. Place in a large pan over a high heat and pour over 1 litre (1¾ pints) of boiling water. Stir in the star anise. Simmer for 25–30 minutes until what looks like unappetising chestnut soup turns into an unappetising grey/brown porridge, encouraging the fruit to disintegrate with a wooden spoon from 15 minutes or so.

Allow to cool a little, then use the spoon to push the pulp – liquid too – through a sieve into a bowl. You are likely to have around 800g (1lb 12oz) purée. Return this to a clean pan and add the sugar and lemon juice. Simmer for 20 minutes or so, stirring once in a while. Don't worry about any froth that rises.

Turn up the temperature and boil for 1 minute before removing from the heat. Stir in the butter (this adds gilt and dispatches the froth) and the ground ginger. Jar immediately

Hazelnuts, chestnuts, Tic Tacs and a stupendous soup

A few days ago, I drove home from a friend's with presents of the best kind: nets of walnuts, hazelnuts and chestnuts slumped on the back seat, like chubby, sleeping grandchildren.

Today, I'll make use of two of them.

At my feet, a snoring, farting dog. Offering yet more evidence of Darwin's theories, he has grown capable of separating the tablet he takes for his slipped disc from the shroud of cheese within which it is presented. An hour or two later, it is not unusual to find a pill – they look like the Tic Tacs of my childhood – secreted in his moustache. Happily, he appears temporarily fooled by a new edible wrapper: a piece of apple served perfectly this morning, though I'm not sure of my chances for this afternoon's medication.

He's bored. No walks allowed, and little freedom to move around as his back legs don't allow him to climb stairs. I carry him from floor to floor to be with one of us; he rests better in company.

Yesterday the sun shone warm and good – the lack of rain felt like a neighbour's strimmer being finally turned off; today, it's throwing it down again. I'm stopping in with the hound.

In the search of warmth and heartiness, I make soup using some of the chestnuts and a Black Futsu squash, with its deep-orange, sweet yet nutty flesh.

While the squash roasts, I'm making hazelnut vodka, a pleasure I first encountered a decade ago thanks to the brilliant forager Liz Knight. Since then, Frangelico – an Italian hazelnut liqueur that's rather heavy on the sweetness but has its uses – has caught my attention, but nothing quite touches a hazelnut vodka made yourself; sugar and spices tweaked to suit.

The dog lifts his head once in a while to snaffle errant hazelnuts that bounce from the table as they're cracked. He's doing ok from it.

He doesn't get so much luck from the chestnuts: the easiest way to tackle them is to cut a slit in each, roast them on a tray for 20–25 minutes, cover them with a tea towel so they steam a little, then peel them when just cool enough to be handled. Their skins grip on tightly to the flesh if they cool too much; if that happens, pop them back in the oven for a couple of minutes. As a guide, it's usual for unshelled, uncooked chestnuts to weigh twice that of them processed, so 400g (14oz) fresh chestnuts gave me the 200g (7oz) of roasted, peeled nuts I needed for the soup.

Squash, leek and chestnut soup

This beauty of a soup sidesteps the usual cooking of onions in a pan, by roasting leeks in the same oven as the squash, bringing a bright leekiness that cuts what – to me at least – can be squash's overbearing sweetness.

This is not as thick as some squash soups, with its flavour eased back and nicely balanced by the leeks, the meatiness of the chestnuts, the bright savoury lemon of the thyme, and the spicy jolt of the harissa. A simple, delicious pleasure.

In a moment of inspiration, I kept a small bit of roasted squash back, in which to hide the dog's pill: his curiosity about a new flavour trumped his suspicion. Today at least, I've won.

MAKES ENOUGH FOR 4, GENEROUSLY

1 squash (about 1kg/2lb 4oz when whole), wedged, seeds removed
6 leeks, green removed, washed
1 litre (1¾ pints) vegetable stock
200g (7oz) cooked chestnuts, roughly chopped
sea salt and freshly ground black pepper

TO SERVE

1 tsp harissa
4 tsp olive oil
few sprigs of lemon thyme, leaves only

Preheat the oven to 200°C/180°C fan/400°F.

Place the squash, cut side up, in a baking tray. Lay the leeks in a separate tray and pop both in the oven. After 15 minutes, check the leeks: when nicely charred, remove and allow them to cool a little.

After a total of 40 minutes, check the squash: it should easily welcome the point of a sharp knife; depending on the variety, it may take a little longer. Allow to cool a little.

Warm the stock in a pan over a medium heat.

Peel the leeks of their most charred outer layers, adding the squeaky centre to a blender, along with half the chestnuts and the flesh of the squash. Add a couple of ladles of stock and blend until completely smooth.

Add the blended soup to a large pan and warm over a medium heat. As it heats through, add as much extra stock as you fancy: I used the entire litre to reach a glorious silkiness, though this can vary depending on the variety of squash. Stir occasionally as the soup warms. Season with salt and pepper as needed.

In a small cup, stir the harissa thoroughly into the oil.

Ladle the soup into bowls, sprinkle with the remaining chestnuts, the lemon thyme leaves and a little black pepper, and drizzle with the harissa oil.

Hazelnut vodka

Depending on your disposition, the dark spectre or warm embrace of Christmas is only just a little out of the headlights' reach. I can hide from it no longer. Make this now as a present to yourself or someone you care about – and you'd better care about them a great deal, as one taste of this and you'll find you care about *yourself* keeping hold of the bottle a very great deal.

MAKES 1 LITRE (1¾ PINTS)

250g (9oz) hazelnuts, giving around 100g (3½oz) shelled
150g (5oz) caster (superfine) sugar
1 litre (1¾ pints) vodka
2 allspice berries, bashed into pieces

Preheat the oven to 190°C/170°C fan/375°F.

Shell the nuts, spread them on a baking tray and pop in the oven for 15 minutes or so, checking after 10: you are after darkened, but not totally black, skins. Wrap the nuts in a tea towel and leave them to steam for a couple of minutes. Rub them through the tea towel, using a combination of scrunching and rolling – this should remove at least half of the skins.

Discard the skins and tip the nuts into a food processor. In short sharp bursts, blitz the nuts into a rubble of varying sizes without much turning to dust.

In a large, wide-mouthed jar, stir the sugar into 200ml (7fl oz) of the vodka until it starts to dissolve. Add the nuts, allspice and the rest of the vodka and stir together.

Leave out of direct sunlight but somewhere you'll see it: you should shake or stir this as near to daily as you remember. The next day it will taste of a special paradise from which you never want to be rescued; after a month it is even more astonishing, and by Christmas you won't want to give it away.

Strain through a fine sieve and/or muslin and funnel into a sterilised bottle/bottles.

Walnuts, Mr Snuffleupagus, fesanjan and the postman's knees

I can no longer see the postman's knees.

The nights may be drawing in, ginkgo leaves fill the gutters and drains, the mulberry may have given its heart-shaped greenery to the soil, but the postman's covered knees are the only sign I'm prepared to accept that it's going to be properly cold.

When I was a kid – when the idea of having a device in your hand that enabled you to watch a match from the other side of the world as it happened was genuinely as fantastical as time travel seems now – postmen never wore shorts. Instead, the start of serious cold was signalled by the headmaster speaking of the life-threatening dangers of placing frozen fingers on a radiator, everyone writing their name against the night sky with sparklers, and – without discussing it – we all went to the chippy rather than the bakery at lunchtime.

The old man would tap the glass of the barometer in the hallway on his way from his chair to his bed; a tilt of the head, a tiny nod, and on he'd go. Every night. Until the night before what was to become the first cold snap, when he would tap the glass of the barometer in the hallway on his way from his chair to his bed, give a tilt of the head, a tiny nod, and utter a small 'hmm' before going on. I'm not convinced that barometer told him anything – or at least anything he understood – but the middle-aged man is little if not the sum of his habits.[1]

Today, I take the mail from the postman's hand while remarking on his hidden knees as my other hand reaches for a net of walnuts I left in the porch.

I grow many things that are all about the punchline. As much as I love beetroot, there isn't much collateral pleasure between marvelling at their beautiful seeds when sowing and picking the roots months later: I'm unlikely to watch the sun set through their leaves while sipping an excellent single malt. Walnuts are different. For two-thirds of the year, walnuts are not far from my mind.

---

1 But now I look back it occurs to me that it was probably a reaction to the weather forecast he watched immediately before turning the telly off and extinguishing his second-to-last cigarette of the day.

When the buds burst, the new spring leaves are a shock of copper and teddy-boy's-socks green, settling down to the more sedate greens of summer into autumn. If you pass a walnut tree, rub one of them: their sweet spiciness crossed with sherbet lemons is one of my most favourite scents. I'm sure there's a liqueur to be made capturing it – perhaps similar to allorino (page 74), the bay leaf infusion from Italy – but I've not heard of anyone making it, and as walnut trees release chemicals which inhibit adjacent plants, it makes me wonder if I might become one of those 'plants' should I drink such a liqueur.

It's easy to miss walnut flowers, at least until you plant a walnut. They carry male and female flowers on the same tree,[2] and quietly beautiful they are too – not in a blousy quince-ish way or in clutches of eye-catching blossom like a pear, but if you have a moment (usually around the FA Cup Final) to approach a walnut tree close enough to say hello, you might see them.

The males hang like Mr Snuffleupagus's nose; the females are less immediately showy, yet even more remarkable close in: their ovaries crowned by two, red antennae stigmas. A few short weeks later, the young shell-less, 'green' walnuts are large enough to harvest for pickling or nocino, both of which are markers in my seasonal calendar.

Having planted 40 walnuts at the old place, I got used to their presence, but our regular-sized garden is too small to accommodate a walnut's greedy reach: thankfully the nearest park has a few grand specimens that – while not hugely productive – carry enough to take a few handfuls of those immature, green walnuts for my kitchen. And a good friend has many at his forest garden in south Devon and is happy for me to buy some: the net in the porch is from him. I very much love that if you keep your eyes open and have some like-minded friends, your virtual garden can make a size way larger than your actual one.

Most of these walnuts will be cracked and prized from their thin shells to enjoy for themselves; the time and palaver involved in shelling a single nut means you can't help but have enough time to savour it while the next is cracked and winkled out.

I've used the rest in fesanjan, a recipe I've been too long since making. Along with one of the Uchiki Kuri squash from the garden and a decent-sized celeriac, a few dozen of these South Devon walnuts found their way into this sweet/sour stew from northern Iran. Commonly made with chicken or lamb, I had a feeling it would really suit this combination of vegetables, and I was right. Sweet, bitter and sour in perfect balance.

2 Generally speaking, walnuts produce more heavily in the presence of a different variety for pollination.

Squash and celeriac fesanjan

One of the pleasures of making this is that the two main elements – the vegetables and the sauce – are cooked separately and brought together at the end, with a few embellishments. While you can dice and cook the celeriac and squash on the hob, in the sauce, the method below allows you to get both just right rather than gamble on them reaching their perfect state together.

Treat the method as a guide, as there is much latitude for variation. Don't worry too much about the exact weight of squash or celeriac; they vary so much in thickness of skin and ratio of flesh to seeds that it doesn't matter too much.

Also, the relative dryness of the nuts, the nature of the molasses, the sweetness of the squash and so on, can all affect the balance of flavour and the amount of stock needed, so taste often and tweak as you like.

For 250g (9oz) of shelled walnuts, you are likely to need around 550g (1lb 4oz) shell-on nuts. Many like to whizz the walnuts to a point where they begin to move from fine powder to oily paste; lovely as this is, I prefer the granularity of something halfway between fine rubble and dust.

SERVES 6

250g (9oz) shelled walnuts
1 good-sized squash, around 1kg (2lb 4oz)
1 good-sized celeriac (celery root), around 1kg (2lb 4oz)
1 tbsp olive oil, plus more to serve
2 tbsp coconut oil
3 onions, halved and thinly sliced
6 garlic cloves, roughly chopped
10cm (4in) cinnamon stick
700ml (1¼ pints) vegetable stock
180ml (6fl oz) pomegranate molasses
10 threads of saffron
1 tbsp salt
2 limes
pinch of sugar (optional)
seeds from ½ pomegranate
freshly grated nutmeg
small handful of coriander (cilantro) leaves, roughly chopped
sea salt and freshly ground black pepper

Pulse the walnuts in a food processor until reduced to a fine rubble.

Preheat the oven to 190°C/170°C fan/375°F.

Cut the squash in half, scoop out and discard the seeds/stringy fibres and cut into wedges. Peel the celeriac and cut these into 2cm (¾in) Jenga blocks. Place the squash, skin side down, in a large baking tray, drizzle the celeriac with olive oil and add that too. Roast for 20–30 minutes until both take the point of a sharp knife with just a little resistance.

While they roast, warm the coconut oil in a medium pan over a lowish heat and cook the onions until soft and translucent, 15 minutes or so. Stir in the garlic and cook for a couple of minutes. Add the cinnamon stick, stock, molasses, saffron and tablespoon of salt and bring to a bare simmer.

Toast the ground walnuts in a large frying pan over a medium heat. Stir semi-constantly, being patient for them to start to turn from biscuit to chocolate brown – once they start it's easy to burn them. Stir them into the oniony stew and gently simmer uncovered for 30 minutes, stirring now and again – you'll see it become glossy as the walnuts release more of their oil. The consistency you are after is 'reluctantly mobile'. Taste and add a little salt and pepper if needed, the juice of half a lime, and a tweak of sugar if it's too sharp.

Spoon the sauce into each bowl, place a wedge or two of squash on each, along with a few sticks of celeriac. Scatter with the pomegranate seeds, squeeze a quarter of a lime over each along with a very generous scratching of nutmeg, a sprinkling of chopped coriander and a swizzle of olive oil.

Serve with flatbreads, rice, or just with greens.

Rose-scented geraniums, lemon verbena, Jeremy Lee and a space hopper

The frost has ridden a space hopper[1] across the garden. What once was perky is now punctuated by soft implosions, browning leaves and crushed stems.

The scented geranium leaves that most enthusiastically reached for the sun suffered most: the youngest, once protected beneath, now exposed. Overnight, the lemon verbena has gone from showing the first sign of eyeliner on its lime green leaves to curling like fried prawns. Winter is making its own compost.

Another hard frost will do for the leaves that remain, so I harvest while I can. Two minutes picking and three snips of the secateurs between heavy downpours and I've enough scented geranium and lemon verbena to last until the plants resprout in late spring. I've left the lemon verbena on the side to dry for the few days they need. Crisp, they retain 90 per cent of their fresh liveliness. That'll do me.

The young, still vibrant, scented geranium leaves need to be dealt with immediately, before they fall quickly into saggy lobes. Half go to herb sugar, half to syrup. This puts them in a kind of culinary holding pattern, their flavour captured to use another time.

Herb sugar

Scented geraniums come in flavours from lemon to lime, hazelnut to pine. Some are a great deal truer to their name than others. Rose is the essential. Tender as they are, they're usually available to buy as plants in late spring, though if grown undercover or in a mild location they can overwinter.

This simple recipe works beautifully with any of the sweeter herbs such as lemon verbena, lavender and mint.

---

1 I must have been nine or so and wanted nothing more than a space hopper. I ached for it in the way Roy Orbison convinced me lost love felt. That Christmas, it arrived. There is no broader smile than the one I wore bouncing down the paths that looped around the houses that sunny, cold Christmas Day afternoon. These short, cold days always remind me of unalloyed, undiluted joy of that Christmas when nothing could improve the world. An Airfix car to make, the *Radio Times* with programmes circled, *The Two Ronnies* had a Christmas special on and the old man even got decent biscuits in for a change.

MAKES 500G (1LB 2OZ)

a couple of dozen rose-scented geranium leaves
500g (1lb 2oz) caster (superfine) sugar

Layer the leaves in the sugar and allow to infuse overnight for a mild flavour, or a week for something more intense. Discard the leaves when using the sugar.

Herb syrup

This couldn't be easier: stir slightly less boiling water by weight into caster sugar – e.g. 250g (9oz) water to 300g (10oz) caster sugar – adding a couple of dozen rose-scented geranium leaves to infuse as it cools.

This is the antithesis of rocket science – the less you add of the herb, the longer the flavour takes to infuse: taste it and sieve out the leaves when it's as you fancy. Bottle and store in the fridge, where it will keep for weeks.

Use on pancakes, poured over ice cream or cakes, in cocktails, with yoghurt, in dressings and so on.

Both the sugar and syrup suit a recipe I've been thinking of since I came home with those bags of nuts the other week. The recipe isn't mine; it's that of an excellent friend, Jeremy Lee.

Jeremy is a car airbag of exuberance, instantly filling the available space with warmth, enthusiasm and Jeremyness. He's a man that should you see him twice a day, you'd still be happy for a third. He writes beautifully, he cooks incredibly and he just makes you feel better about the world. He is, as Jay Rayner remarked, 'one of those rare phenomena in the London food world: a chap everyone agrees is a good thing.'[2]

I made his walnut cake a long time ago, but for reasons unknown and insubstantial – given how special it is – not since. I borrowed it today, inspired by that net of hazelnuts and the rose-scented geraniums. Nuts, rose, sugar: a baklava combination I hoped might translate to his cake, and it most certainly does.

2 *Guardian*, 11 March 2012

Hazelnut and rose cake

My recipe differs from Jeremy's in a few respects: for example, I use 5 medium eggs to his 4 large; I employ hazelnuts in place of walnuts; I like slightly more olive oil; I've added rosiness, and so on – but I mean no disrespect, only gratitude.

There are two ways to make this: as below, or – if you've made the syrup – knock back the sugar to 175g (6oz), halve the quantity of oil and (having made numerous holes with a cake skewer) drizzle some of the syrup over the cake as it cools and allow it to soak in.

SERVES 6

5 eggs, separated
40ml (1½fl oz) olive oil
225g (8oz) rose sugar (or use caster/superfine sugar and 2 tsp rose water)
350g (12oz) shelled hazelnuts, coarsely ground
finely grated zest of 1 lemon
icing (confectioner's) sugar, for dusting (optional)

Preheat the oven to 180°C/160°C fan/350°F and line a 23cm (9in) cake tin with baking parchment.

Beat the egg yolks, oil and sugar together until pale and fluffy. Fold in the hazelnuts and lemon zest.

In another bowl, whisk the egg whites to form soft peaks. Fold a third through the nutty, oily egg mix until combined, then carefully fold in the remaining egg whites.

Pour into the cake tin. Place in the centre of the oven and bake for 40 minutes. Test with a skewer or similar and allow a few minutes longer if needed.

Dust with icing sugar if you like. Serve with whatever kind of cream makes you happiest.

Salsify, Rik Mayall, radicchio and a winter gratin

The bath might be my favourite place. While it seems half the world submerges in freezing water for spiritual uplift, I crave warm bones, digits like sponge fingers, a little while with an empty brain, and a chapter or two of a good book.

A couple of decades ago, that book was very often *Jane Grigson's Vegetable Book*, or her *Fruit Book*, both of which gave me so many ideas about what to grow and what to do with it in the kitchen. What is a medlar? Are Chinese artichokes any good?

The first year I grew anything, her description of salsify and its dark-skinned sister scorzonera had me searching for the then pretty obscure seed. Sown the following spring, they germinated quickly enough but took a long, warm season to drive long thin roots into the soil, fattening – as much as they ever do – close to Bonfire Night, making the newcomer gardener anxious as to whether they'd come to much. I learned that they thrive in a good deep, ideally light soil where the roots can grow to 30 or even 40cm; I also learned that they still taste as good grown in a heavier soil where the root splits like a joke cigar. You have to use a fork to lift and loosen them: pull on the leafy end as you might a carrot, and you'll end up – as I did – with a stump in your hand and a muddy arse.

In this rainiest of weeks, when two baths a day wouldn't seem unreasonable, I took the *Vegetable Book* to the tub again. What a voice Grigson had. Forthright but friendly, definite yet approachable. She oozes authority and her recipes live up to it. I love her economy, assuming the reader has common sense.

She reminds me that the flavoursome but sturdy wild scorzonera was improved by Italian gardeners, a more succulent root the result. It came to the UK unspecifically, well before the paler salsify's arrival 300 years ago. But… 'the odd thing is that neither has ever really caught on, at least with the general public. Intelligent gardeners, from John Evelyn onwards, have always grown either salsify or scorzonera.'

I wonder if – along with the apparent deliciousness – it was that phrase 'intelligent gardeners' that was responsible for me first growing it? There's nothing like a bit of implied flattery to seduce a man who has no idea what he's doing.

Salsify's flavour is a mix of artichoke hearts, asparagus and the scent of a distant seashore. You can skin them before boiling but it's a faff: a fair bit of flesh is lost to the peeler, and they need submerging in acidulated water to prevent discolouring. Instead, I simmer the washed roots until al dente and plunge them into cold water, and the skins need only the gentlest persuasion from a dinner knife to slide off.

Happily, the seeds and the roots are more widely available than they were.

One of the things I love most about salsify and scorzonera is that if you don't get around to harvesting them all, they flower like purple chimney brushes the following year. The seed heads that follow are similarly beautiful. I almost always leave at least a few; once or twice, I've even sown a swathe for the flowers and seed alone.

As with salsify and scorzonera, it is bitter leaves' time of year.

My wife grows radicchio. These deeply purple- and green-leaved chicories form a semi-tight ball, as if the leaves were half-heartedly papier-mâchéd. I love them for their looks as much as their flavour. Once the seedlings are planted out, life means they are largely left to fend for themselves, and sure enough – as ever – the love they have in those first few weeks is enough to see them through.

A quarter of a century ago, I had no enthusiasm for the bitterness of radicchio, pointed chicory or endive until I took a big, pale, blousy, frilly-as-a-dolly's-skirt endive and fried it whole in a wok with just a little spitting oil to stop it sticking to the blistering pan. An assault of salt and pepper and a honey mustard dressing had me converted.

Bitter leaves like a little sweetness or the comfort of dairy to sort them out; the French typically throw butter, cream and cheese at salsify, so I hoped a gratin of the two might just work. And it really does.

Salsify and radicchio gratin

This is utterly adaptable to those avoiding dairy or gluten: I used gluten-free plain flour, and I've used both dairy and their plant-based alternatives; both are delicious. You can use either large, round radicchio cut into wedges or pointed chicory cut in half lengthways. I know many love a cheesy gratin and I won't deny its appeal, but sometimes the flavour of the vegetables deserves just the touch of cream and an over-enthusiasm of nutmeg rather than the (often welcome) Lord Flashheart that something like Taleggio brings.

SERVES 6

600g (1lb 5oz) salsify, top and tailed
600g (1lb 5oz) radicchio, sliced into wedges
1 tbsp olive oil
40g (1½oz) butter
40g (1½oz) plain (all-purpose) flour
400ml (14fl oz) milk
180ml (6fl oz) double (heavy) cream
2 tbsp English mustard
¼ nutmeg
very generous pinch of smoked paprika
sea salt and freshly ground black pepper

Preheat the oven to 200°C/180°C fan/400°F.

Simmer the salsify in a large pan of water for 15–20 minutes until it takes the point of a sharp knife easily. Drain. Remove the skin with a dinner knife and discard.

In a large frying pan, over a medium heat, fry the radicchio wedges in olive oil, turning as needed, until nicely browned and tender.

Meanwhile, in a small pan, cook the butter and flour together over a medium heat for a couple of minutes until it bubbles, then whisk in the milk a little at a time until fully incorporated. Gradually add the cream, whisking constantly. Cook for a few minutes, stirring often, then add the mustard and season well with salt and pepper.

Place the salsify in a 20 x 30cm (8 x 12in) gratin dish, set the radicchio on top and pour over the sauce. Grate nutmeg over the top, sprinkle with smoked paprika and bake for about 20 minutes until golden. Serve with something green and squeaky: sprouts, tenderstem, sprouting broccoli or lamb's lettuce.

Pall Mall, mooli, James Dean and kimchi

I am sat on the step by the shed, the sodden ground dipping away from my feet towards the house. The dog has left his morning present somewhere, a somewhere that no amount of walking around has identified. I'm hoping that sitting still and scanning might reveal it; a game of battleships no one wants to play.

I miss smoking. When sat still like this, a small part of me still reaches for the tobacco – that twin I'd never let out of my sight, now replaced by the phone. I miss the palaver of rolling a cigarette, the smell of the petrol lighter, the letterbox of card holding the papers. Back when smoking was good for you, it was perfectly acceptable – encouraged even – to stop what you were doing for a cigarette. You could barely start something before you paused for a puff.

I miss the punctuation it brought.

When you're a kid, life is broken into manageable slices of contrasting time. Wake up, breakfast, go to school, play, lessons, play, lunch, play, pinch matey's Sherbet Dip-Dab, lessons, play, get deadlegged by matey for pinching his Sherbet Dip-Dab, lessons, home, play, tea, play, bed. Term starts, term ends, half term starts, half term ends, second half of term begins, Christmas holidays start, and on it goes. Time felt rich, yet passed slowly; it felt like a decade between birthdays.

Go to work and smoking broke the day into pleasing chunks again. It made you stop. It also lifted you above suspicion: stand around doing nothing and you were a sex pest or burglar; do nothing but puff on a Pall Mall and you became James Dean.[1] Like walking does now, smoking occupied my brain just enough to stop it looking for something to do, and as a result things fell into its unoccupied territory. Rollie to hand, I could happily sit within an album's landscape, every note and word registering; now, I find it hard to submit to even the finest listen without reaching for my phone once in a while.

The trouble with breaking the day up with smoking is what you gain on the punctuating swing, you lose on the heart attack roundabout. Given that I carry the genes of a predisposition to early-onset heart disease, and spent the first quarter century of my life either inhaling the old man's smoke or my own, it might be wise to stack my punctuating chips on a different colour.

1 'Why do we do this?' 'You gotta do something' is a great bit of dialogue.

I think I may have accidentally found it. No, not playing dogshit battleships.

The kettle packed in. I found a stovetop one in a box in storage. It takes an age to boil. No more running downstairs at 4 minutes to Zoom o'clock and back with a drink in time to catch the start. It does have one thing in its favour, though: an impressive whistle.

The kettle is conspiring with the book.

One of the joys of writing this book live, week by bit, is how the garden and cooking have become even more embedded in my life. It has given me more of a reason to look, observe and listen when life, deadlines, slow mood, admin and other tediums might otherwise get in the way. I take pictures every day, I make more films, I record sound clips. I taste and smell things out there more days than not.

The kettle's slowness is providing me with yet another excuse to step into the garden when I light the flame. It might only take 10 minutes for it to come to a whistling boil and signal the need for my return, but taking that time outside a few times a day while I wait (rather than absentmindedly stroking the glass hamster)[2] is surprisingly rewarding.

Despite the rain, this morning's 10 minutes meant I went outside when I might not have; I lifted the foliage of the mooli to inspect what I presumed would be parsnip-sized mooli, and was mightily surprised. Mooli – aka daikon – is a large radish, of sorts. Particularly well loved in Japan, it takes brilliantly to pickling, stir fries, being chopped as a crudité, coleslawed and so much more; if you like radish you are very likely to love mooli. And, as it turns out, a programme of disinterest, busyness and a functioning kettle has had them growing beautifully from a mid-summer sowing. The combination of a new bed full of fresh compost and a rainy year has fed the plants to such a size that two-thirds of each is above ground. Despite frosts, winds and rain, the foliage still looks fresh. The mooli themselves look beautiful: my worry was for the flavour and the texture. Would they be woody? Are they hotter than July?

Happily, this single monster is 1.869g of crisp, cool, juicy deliciousness without a hint of woodiness and just a distant hint of pepper, as you'd want.

Another week of rain, deadlines, distraction and a functioning electric kettle and I might have missed the mooli flourishing, hidden under their foliage. So the slow kettle – with its excuse to pause and punctuate in such a way as to not shorten my life – stays.[3]

2 I owe my good pal Valentine Warner for his excellent description of scrolling on your phone.
3 I found that present from the hound by the raised bed where the mooli were growing, of course.

Mooli kimchi

Great in pickles, mooli are similarly splendid when fermented, and this kimchi is my default core recipe for a fish-free, lively celebration of what's in season. I've made versions of this with a quarter of the radish switched out for red grapefruit, using half Chinese leaf to radish, and with a mix of fruit; the key thing is the proportion of salt. It has to be 2 per cent by weight in order to discourage harmful bacteria, create the ideal conditions for beneficial bacteria to proliferate (bringing huge benefits to our gut biome) and not be too salty for deliciousness.

By all means make this with radishes, carrots, Chinese leaf (as is traditional) or other crisp vegetable of your liking.

MAKES ABOUT 700G (1½LB)

600g (1lb 5oz) washed, peeled mooli
12g (½oz) fine sea salt
5 spring onions (scallions)
4 garlic cloves
5cm (2in) knob of ginger, peeled
20g (¾oz) Korean chilli powder

Either thinly slice or – as I do here – use a peeler to create thin ribbons of mooli. Place in a large bowl and combine with the salt, mixing well.

Slice the spring onions thinly, and either finely chop or use a fine microplane to reduce the garlic and ginger to a mush. Add this all to the mooli, along with the chilli powder, and mix well.

Spoon the mixture into a 700ml (1¼-pint) – or larger – Kilner jar, pressing down carefully to squeeze out any air bubbles. Use a pickle pebble or food bag partly filled with water to keep the ribbons submerged. Seal the jar.

Allow the kimchi to ferment for 2 weeks at room temperature, burping the jar every day or two. Taste it after a few days and then every couple of days to become familiar with how the flavour develops. Transfer the jar to the fridge when it has the flavour and sourness you like.

Whispering death, Scooby Doo, a balsa-wood barge and lebkuchen

There is a day on which everyone discovers their dad is a nutter.

Mine came aged 11, midsummer, at a friend's house. Two hours playing cricket in the farmyard – a milk churn for the wicket, my friend England, me the West Indies[1] – came to a close when the midday sun sent us indoors for cheese sandwiches and cold pop. On the kitchen table, a jar of piccalilli.

'Left over from Christmas?' I asked.

'What?'

'The piccalilli… left over from Christmas?'

'What are you talking about?'

'Piccalilli… it's a Christmas thing!' I scoffed.

'What are you talking about!'

This was the first crack in a façade that quickly spread – as if in a Scooby Doo earthquake – into the widest of canyons.

It became apparent that – rather than it being a convention upheld by the rest of civilisation – it was only my old man who considered walnuts, Turkish Delight, Ritz biscuits, After Eights, ginger cordial, dates and piccalilli just for Christmas.

Further festive madnesses walked out of the childhood mist: I've no idea why he bought a balsa-wood barge of dates when neither he nor I (nor the cat) liked them. A bottle of Mateus Rosé – looking (and indeed tasting) as if it had spent centuries lost at sea before washing up on our doorstep – opened with Christmas lunch, a small glass taken, the rest ignored for weeks before vanishing without warning or ceremony. Ginger cordial, the colour of caramel, he drank neat; a sippable inch in a glass as if it were a single malt – I did the same, assuming that's how it was. He lifted After Eights from their dark green

---

1 If there is a more graceful sight in sport than Michael Holding (aka 'Whispering Death') bowling, I have yet to see it.

box, replacing the envelope in a serial-killer move that gave the impression to his young son that there were still many left to eat. It was like reaching for a favourite record and finding no vinyl inside.

As a kid, there were only three spices in the house: white pepper,[2] ragingly hot dried chillies, and a short jar of mixed spice that arrived soon after the first supermarket opened and sat unused – warm spices in a cold larder – after my mum left.

The old man was born in Sri Lanka and spent his first 13 years living in the sun; a life of warm winds, luscious fruit and glinting seas. I'm not sure he ever got over leaving. He wasn't such a cook. His curries were – with the occasional leftover chicken or Boxing Day turkey variation – cheap mince and onions fried without mercy in a generous berg of lard lifted from the chip pan with the point of The Sharp Knife, spiced only with white pepper and an assault of dried chillies kept in an old Nescafé jar. Even from my bedroom, I could pick up the moment the white pepper was deployed: no air rises quicker than that peppered air rose from the pan up the stairs and – somehow – through my closed bedroom door. Even now, few smells make me as hungry as white pepper hitting hot fat.

Christmases now are still very much about spices, only – thankfully – more of them than the three of my childhood. Cloves in the bread sauce, star anise in the mulled cider, nutmeg on the roast potatoes (if you don't, you should), nutmeg on the sprouts (if you don't, you should), warming spices in mince pies and Christmas pudding etc., etc.

Every December, I make lebkuchengewürz – a classic German spice blend – and for this year's batch I'm using the last stick of a batch of cinnamon – a gift from a lovely person – grown on the island she was visiting: Sri Lanka, home of cinnamon and the old man. And a few white peppercorns that, surprisingly, make it even better.

---

2 There was a weekend somewhere in the late '70s when everything changed: pasta and duvets came to Britain, and everyone swapped from white to black pepper.

Lebkuchengewürz

This German gingerbread spice blend on or in anything makes the house smell of Christmas: if you do nothing but keep it in a jar to inhale once a day, life will be improved. A three-fingered pinch over rice pudding, dusted over hot chocolate or when making gingerbread will see you very right.

This is heavier on the mace and cardamom than I often go for: for reasons unknown it is just what I feel like this year. I love how the spices reveal themselves independently, the cloves first and lastly the mace heading to the shops when you're already coming back with the change.

MAKES A SMALL JAR

6cm (2½in) cinnamon stick
10 cloves
10 allspice berries
2 skeletons of mace
seeds from 16 cardamom pods
½ tsp ginger
4 white peppercorns (optional)
1 tsp anise seed (or fennel if you have no anise)

Place everything in a coffee/spice grinder or a mortar and pestle and reduce to a fine-ish powder. Store in a jar.

Lebkuchen

These German festive biscuits are easy and special, and while they cook and cool, the house will be perfumed with the scent of Christmas. For the gluten intolerant, you can use gluten-free plain flour or a mix of oat flour and ground almonds; the icing sugar and cocoa are untraditional and non-essential, but I like them nevertheless.

Whatever you do, don't overcook lebkuchen: their texture should be somewhere between firm and not, and too much heat makes them less satisfying.

Rather than irritate myself with the faff of using a cookie cutter, I've taken to rolling up the mix into a couple of 5cm (2in) fat sausages, wrapping each in greaseproof and freezing them to slice into 1cm (½in) thick coins and cook from frozen when I fancy: they form low, wide drumlins of just the right dimensions to encourage the ideal mix of soft to crunch.

MAKES ABOUT 30

150ml (5fl oz) honey
60g (2¼oz) unsalted butter, softened
2 large eggs
450g (1lb) plain (all-purpose) flour
2 tbsp lebkuchengewürz
3 good pinches of salt
½ tsp baking powder
½ tsp bicarbonate of soda (baking soda)
170g (6oz) soft dark brown sugar
finely grated zest of 1 lemon
icing (confectioner's) sugar, for dusting
cocoa powder, for dusting

Pour the honey and butter into a small pan and warm over a low heat, stirring to combine.

Briefly whisk the eggs in a cup. Put the remaining ingredients in a bowl and stir in the honey butter. Slowly add the eggs and stir in: a tacky dough should come together.

At this point, either roll into sausages, freeze and cut fat draughts to cook when you fancy them, or proceed as below.

Cover the bowl with a damp tea towel and place in the fridge for an hour.

Preheat the oven to 180°C/160°C fan/350°F and line 2–3 baking sheets with baking parchment.

Lightly dust the work surface and roll the dough out to around 7–8mm (¼in) thick. Use a cookie cutter to make biscuits of whatever shape you favour. Lay the cut biscuit dough on the baking trays and bake for about 12 minutes until very slightly risen: catch them before they darken too much. Cool on a wire rack before dusting with icing sugar and cocoa. They will store for 4–5 days in an airtight container.

David Mitchell, Japanese quince, the Helford and a confused bee

I'm not one for living in the moment. Much of the reason I love these days that belong to neither Christmas nor New Year is that they are often happily reflective, with so many of the festive rituals ringing bells from other times.

Fourteen Christmases ago, my daughter was lying in her bed being read to by her mother. I was in the next room reading about pecans and how – in sweet increments of success and failure – they'd made the long trip north from the river basins of the southern states of America into Canada. Gradually, gradually, over generations and centuries, adventurous smallholders intent on growing their own had taken seedlings from the most northerly pecans and planted them a mile or two up the road in the hope they'd acclimatise.

I liked that spirit of inquisitive gardening. The smallholding I'd begun from two bare east Devon fields was filling with hundreds of species, many unusual or even unique in this country – almonds, Nepalese pepper, Asian pears, American persimmons and more – and had some of that same feeling.

My daughter called me in. Trent, a fine man who had worked with me in the 3½-acre vineyard I'd planted, had crossed the pond and we were all missing him.

'Where is Trent, Dad?'

'Here.' I lifted her new globe and pointed to where Trent was. 'He's near a place called Bellingham, just north of Seattle, close to the top of the United States.'

'And where are we?'

I pointed to us on the globe. 'Here we are, bean, right here.'

I moved my finger between the two, spinning the globe to show we were – at least to the accuracy of a grown-up's finger – at the same level on the globe.

'We're here and he's there.'

A penny dropped.

I tucked her in before going back to my office to google 'pecan nurseries, Canada', the globe still spinning in my mind between two points on similar latitude.

A couple of months later, 40 young seedlings arrived. I planted them over a weekend, close to the river of this southern state of the UK in the hope it reminded them of home.

Five years later, making my own gravy under the high summer sun, I sat against the thickest trunk, cool under the canopy. It occurred to me that I might be the first person on these islands to have sat in a pecan orchard, being shaded by one of its trees. And that, peculiar as that realisation felt, I owed that feeling to hundreds, perhaps thousands, of smallholders and inquisitive gardeners, a huge ocean away, who had given the uncertain a try.

It is perhaps the thing I love most about growing: the connection to those enthusiastic others who improved, moved, communicated or planted what now gives pleasure. That connection can happen on the smallest scale.

Below the dining room window, in a quiet corner of our small garden, grows a Chaenomeles – known variously as the flowering quince, Japanese quince and more – planted by the previous owner. Chaenomeles generally grow low and wide,[1] flowering like crazy through spring. It is most definitely not March, neither is it April, yet it thinks it is. A bee just stopped by the window – perhaps it too was confused by the plant flowering while carrying the previous year's fruit. If ever we needed a sign of what's coming, here is a small and striking one.

Along and beneath the tangle of spiky stems, are little clusters of green and yellow fruit. Hard as a hammer, the fallen quince brought together by the stony contours of the bed are undamaged. Their perfume is similar to tree quince, though I find their scent spicier; similar to walnut leaves' sherbet fruitiness. It's impossible not to lift each one to your nose.

As with the more familiar quince, Chaenomeles fruit require warmth and/or sweetness to give up their charms.

---

1 There is one by a house on the walk from home to the sea that stands like a low apple, the fruit seemingly unharvested. I want to knock on their door and tell them that they have something special to the side of the gate that I imagine they struggle through, bags of shopping in hand, unaware of what they let go uneaten.

Grate them into a large jar of vodka or gin and sweeten with an inch of sugar and the liqueur that results from a couple of months of steeping will make you very happy. I've made enough of those kind of infusions this year, so these made jelly.

And what a jelly.

This morning, in Cornwall with excellent friends we often share the turn of the year with, and ahead of a morning's walk, I made that favourite porridge for seven. Porridge can be the worst of risotto-alikes without toppings: here, pumpkin and sunflower seeds, tahini, cream, an indecent amount of nutmeg, and a generous scoop of perhaps the best jelly I've ever made.

It fuelled us for a three-hour loop of the southern bank of the mouth of the Helford; a perfect window of sunshine and calm in an otherwise stormy spell.

Seven happy people will leave with a jar of that jelly, the taste perhaps reminding them of a sunny Christmas walk, another link in that chain of pleasure started by the person who planted that young bush under our dining room window.

Japanese quince jelly with star anise and white pepper

The weight of fruit doesn't really matter – this is all about proportions – though if it helps to plan likely quantities, I had 3kg (6lb 12oz) fruit and used 2kg (4lb 8oz) sugar (I used 3:1 caster to light brown).

I saw a recipe from the excellent food writer Christine McFadden[2] some time ago that suggested including pink peppercorns; my festive obsession with white pepper had me trying it in half the batch and it is SO good that I encourage you to consider the peppercorns as essential rather than optional.

Japanese quince
sugar
lemon juice
star anise
white peppercorns, crushed (optional)

2 Her book *Pepper* is very, very good.

Chop the quince into quarters; and in half again for larger fruit.

Place in a large pan, just cover with water and bring to the boil. Reduce the heat and simmer for 40 minutes or so until soft.

Tie a jelly bag or large square of muslin over a large bowl – I use an upturned chair – ensuring the muslin is held well clear of the bowl.

Ladle the fruit purée into the bag. Allow to drain overnight. Avoid squeezing the bag unless you prefer cloudy jelly.

Weigh the liquid. In a large pan over a medium heat – a preserving pan is ideal – add an equal weight of sugar to liquid, plus the juice of 1 lemon, 2 star anise and ½ teaspoon of white pepper (if using) for every 500g (1lb 2oz) of liquid, and stir with a long-handled spoon until dissolved.

Increase the heat and boil until the temperature reaches 105°C (220°F) on a sugar thermometer.[3] When everything gets a bit excitable, carefully agitate the centre of the pan with the spoon and it will calm a little.

A froth will appear, like a pure white crust on a brûlée: keep a bowl handy so you can skim and discard it.

Add a little very hot water to each sterilised jar to prepare it for accepting the hot jelly; tip out the water and pour or ladle the jelly into each.

3 Or until a teaspoonful wrinkles like cellulite when dropped on a chilled plate.

Here I am, 52 weeks older than when I started writing what would become this book.

For no conscious reason, I've driven to my hometown beach just around the coast. The sea is a Farrow and Ball olive, the rain throwing itself to the ground, the wind scratching at clothes, birds and buildings, and running the sea in shallow fast waves across the grain of the tide. The gentle rocking of the car is the wind telling me how cold it is, and I am prepared to believe it.

I'm often pleasingly troubled by revisiting old places. Finding elements exactly as they were – the rough surface of the seawall in front of the car marked exactly as in the photo, taken perhaps 70 years ago, of the old man suited, his foot on that exact spot, his pushbike still, drawing on one of the fags that 40 years later would hasten him to an early grave.

It feels as if I am staring at a cartoon, with only my lacking in understanding of how it might occur stopping me drawing that past into the now, or the now into the past. I guess that's what writing is for.

I've taken a longer, more complete break over Christmas than usual and I realise that these last few days had me wondering if I had lost the ability, perhaps even the urge, to write.

I realise that writing has quietly become like a fifth limb, a sixth taste, another sense by which I understand myself and the world, and that I can only go so long without writing before I feel detached; perhaps incapable of being most fully who I am. As Geoff Nicholson wrote in *The Lost Art of Walking*, 'Writing is one way of making the world our own and… walking is another.' Amen.

Today I am here. Today I showed up and words have fallen out of me, as they have done every week for the past year. I hope you've enjoyed them. Thank you for showing up too. Maybe that worry that I'd lost the words was because I knew the year was up, and perhaps I needed to come here to realise that I shouldn't stop just because those 52 weeks had come to a close.

Here's to another year of an abundance of living, eating, writing and paying attention more fully than the one before. I hope for you too.

Mark
markdiacono.substack.com

Index

A

Alexanders ice cream
69–71
allorino: blackberry
allorino 74
Wonka's allorino 73
allspice: ginger and allspice
olive oil cake with
double ginger rhubarb
41–3
apple and blackberry
brown betty crumble
198–201
apricots: sweet cicely
apricots, yoghurt and
mugolio 125–6
artichokes: vignarola 121–3
asparagus: asparagus and
sauce gribiche on toast
86
asparagus and spring
onion frittata 80
sprouting broccoli,
asparagus and spring
flower gratin 90
vignarola 121–3
aubergines (eggplants):
baba ganoush 166

B

baba ganoush 166
bay flowers: Wonka's
allorino 73
bay leaves: blackberry
allorino 74
beans, Devon spiced 238
biscuits: lebkuchen 270–2
bitters, Seville orange 26–7
blackberries: apple and
blackberry brown betty
crumble 198–201
blackberry allorino 74
blackberry whisky 201
honeyed blackberry
vinegar 203

late summer fruit
panzanella 175–6
Bloody Mary 181
Bonnington tortilla 159–61
borlotti beans: Devon
spiced beans 238
boulangère, potato and
celeriac 57–9
bread: apple and
blackberry brown betty
crumble 198–201
asparagus and sauce
gribiche on toast 86
onion seed and oregano
flower focaccia 219–20
tomatoes on toast with
tomato leaf pistou
180–1
brioche: late summer fruit
panzanella 175–6
broad bean leaf and lemon
risotto 110–12
broad beans: early summer
shakshuka 135–7
vignarola 121–3
brown betty crumble,
apple and blackberry
198–201
burrata: early summer
shakshuka 135–7
fig, watercress and
burrata salad with
honey and fennel
dressing 206
butter beans: chard,
celery, butter bean and
tarragon stew with
celery and tarragon
pesto 35–7

C

cakes: ginger and allspice
olive oil cake with
double ginger rhubarb
41–3

hazelnut and rose cake
257
capers: sauce gribiche 85–6
caraway seeds: cranberry
and caraway flapjack
32
cardoon gratin 99
carrots: panch phoran
roast carrots with green
goddess dressing 66
cauliflower and sage soup
23
cedar cones: mugolio 103
celeriac: potato and celeriac
boulangère 57–9
squash and celeriac
fesanjan 251–2
celery: chard, celery, butter
bean and tarragon
stew with celery and
tarragon pesto 35–7
chana chaaty salad, cherry
189
chard, celery, butter bean
and tarragon stew with
celery and tarragon
pesto 35–7
cheese: broad bean leaf and
lemon risotto 110–12
cardoon gratin 99
early summer shakshuka
135–7
fig, watercress and
burrata salad with
honey and fennel
dressing 206
pan haggerty 217
cherries: cherry and
coriander seed clafoutis
131–2
cherry chana chaaty salad
189
pickled cherries 132
chestnuts: squash, leek and
chestnut soup 245–7

chickpeas: cherry chana
chaaty salad 189
hummus 168
Chinese five spice 222–3
chocolate: hazelnut and
chocolate cookies 54
clafoutis, cherry and
coriander seed 131–2
coconut milk: fig leaf and
olive oil ice cream 155
The Rupert Holmes 108
coleslaw: fennel, rhubarb
and radish coleslaw
with elderflower
dressing 46–7
cookies, hazelnut and
chocolate 54
cordials: the best
elderflower cordial 116
lime flower cordial 147–8
coriander seeds: cherry and
coriander seed clafoutis
131–2
cornichons: sauce gribiche
85–6
cranachan: mulberry
cranachan 171–2
squash cranachan 233
cranberry and caraway
flapjack 32
cream: Alexanders ice
cream 69–71
gooseberry and
strawberry Eton mess
143–4
mulberry cranachan
171–2
sprouting broccoli,
asparagus and spring
flower gratin 90
squash cranachan 233
twice baked potatoes
with rosemary creamed
leeks and smoked
paprika 211–12

crumble: apple and
blackberry brown
betty crumble 198–201
fig and fennel crumble
224
curd, squash 232–3

D
Devon spiced beans 238
dips: baba ganoush 166
hummus 168
dressings: elderflower
dressing 46–7
grapefruit and
elderflower dressing
207
green goddess dressing
64
honey and fennel
dressing 206
drinks: the best
elderflower cordial 116
blackberry allorino 74
Bloody Mary 181
elderflower gin 115
elderflower martini 115
gooseberry and
elderflower shrub
126–9
gorse flower piña colada
108
gorse flower rum 106
hazelnut vodka 248
lime flower cordial
147–8
mulberry martini 172
rhubarb and lovage
gimlet 94
The Rupert Holmes 108
Seville orange bitters
26–7
Seville orange spiced
rum 28
a summer Tom Collins
148
Wonka's allorino 73

E
early summer shakshuka
135–7
eggs: Alexanders ice
cream 69–71

asparagus and spring
onion frittata 80
Bonnington tortilla
159–61
early summer
shakshuka 135–7
fig leaf and olive oil ice
cream 155
sauce gribiche 85–6
squash curd 232–3
elderflower cordial:
elderflower dressing
46–7
gooseberry and
elderflower shrub
126–9
gooseberry and
strawberry Eton mess
143–4
grapefruit and
elderflower dressing
207
elderflower gin 115
elderflower martini 115
elderflowers: the best
elderflower cordial 116
elderflower gin 115
gooseberry and
elderflower shrub
G&T 129
Eton mess, gooseberry and
strawberry 143–4

F
fennel, rhubarb and
radish coleslaw with
elderflower dressing
46–7
fennel seeds: fig and
fennel crumble 224
honey and fennel
dressing 206
fesanjan, squash and
celeriac 251–2
fig leaves: fig leaf and
olive oil ice cream 155
fig leaf syrup 154
figs: fig and fennel
crumble 224
fig, watercress and
burrata salad with
honey and fennel
dressing 206

flapjack, cranberry and
caraway 32
focaccia, onion seed and
oregano flower 219–20
frittata, asparagus and
spring onion 80
fruit: late summer fruit
panzanella 175–6

G
G&T, gooseberry and
elderflower shrub 129
garlic: early summer
shakshuka 135–7
fresh tomato, runner
bean and tarragon
pasta 186–9
squash and celeriac
fesanjan 251–2
vignarola 121–3
gimlet, rhubarb and
lovage 94
gin: elderflower gin 115
gooseberry and
elderflower shrub
G&T 129
mulberry martini 172
rhubarb and lovage
gimlet 94
a summer Tom Collins
148
Wonka's allorino 73
ginger: double ginger
rhubarb 41–3
ginger and allspice olive
oil cake with double
ginger rhubarb 41–3
ginger beer: Seville orange
wintry mojito 28
gingerbread spice mix:
lebkuchengewürz 270
gooseberries: gooseberry
and elderflower shrub
126–9
gooseberry and
strawberry Eton mess
143–4
gooseberry and
elderflower shrub
126–9
gooseberry and
elderflower shrub
G&T 129

gorse flowers: gorse flower
rum 106
gorse flower syrup 106
The Rupert Holmes 108
grapefruit juice:
grapefruit and
elderflower dressing
207
gratins: cardoon gratin 99
salsify and radicchio
gratin 262
sprouting broccoli,
asparagus and spring
flower gratin 90
green goddess dressing 64
panch phoran roast
carrots with green
goddess dressing 66
Gruyère: cardoon gratin
99

H
harira soup, squash 230–2
hazelnuts: hazelnut and
chocolate cookies 54
hazelnut and rose cake
257
hazelnut butter 51
hazelnut vodka 248
herbs: herb sugar 254–5
herb syrup 255
honey: honey and fennel
dressing 206
honeyed blackberry
vinegar 203
hummus 168

I
ice cream: Alexanders ice
cream 69–71
fig leaf and olive oil ice
cream 155

J
Japanese quince jelly with
star anise and white
pepper 275–6

K
kimchi, mooli 266

L

late summer fruit panzanella 175–6

lebkuchen 270–2

lebkuchengewürz 270

leeks: sprouting broccoli, asparagus and spring flower gratin 90

squash harira soup 230–2

squash, leek and chestnut soup 245–7

tomato and rosemary soup 195–6

twice baked potatoes with rosemary creamed leeks and smoked paprika 211–12

lemons: the best elderflower cordial 116

broad bean leaf and lemon risotto 110–12

lime flower cordial 147–8

a summer Tom Collins 148

lentils: squash harira soup 230–2

lime flower cordial 147–8

a summer Tom Collins 148

lovage: rhubarb and lovage gimlet 94

M

martini: elderflower martini 115

mulberry martini 172

mayonnaise: green goddess dressing 64

medlar thing 242

meringues: gooseberry and strawberry Eton mess 143–4

milk: Alexanders ice cream 69–71

mirabelles: late summer fruit panzanella 175–6

mojito, Seville orange wintry 28

mooli kimchi 266

mugolio 103

sweet cicely apricots, yoghurt and mugolio 125–6

mulberries: mulberry cranachan 171–2

mulberry martini 172

N

nectarines: late summer fruit panzanella 175–6

New Year porridge 14

nut butter: hazelnut butter 51

nuts: New Year porridge 14

sweet cicely apricots, yoghurt and mugolio 125–6

O

oat milk: New Year porridge 14

oats: apple and blackberry brown betty crumble 198–201

cranberry and caraway flapjack 32

fig and fennel crumble 224

hazelnut and chocolate cookies 54

mulberry cranachan 171–2

New Year porridge 14

squash cranachan 233

olive oil: fig leaf and olive oil ice cream 155

ginger and allspice olive oil cake with double ginger rhubarb 41–3

sauce gribiche 85–6

onion seed and oregano flower focaccia 219–20

onions: Bonnington tortilla 159–61

pan haggerty 217

quick pickled onions 207

oranges: Seville orange bitters 26–7

Seville orange spiced rum 28

Seville orange wintry mojito 28

oregano flowers: onion seed and oregano flower focaccia 219–20

P

pan haggerty 217

panch phoran roast carrots with green goddess dressing 66

panzanella, late summer fruit 175–6

Parmesan: broad bean leaf and lemon risotto 110–12

pistou 178–80

pasta: fresh tomato, runner bean and tarragon pasta 186–9

squash harira soup 230–2

peas: early summer shakshuka 135–7

rainy summer day pea and tarragon soup 151

vignarola 121–3

pepper, Japanese quince jelly with star anise and white 275–6

pesto: celery and tarragon pesto 35–7

tomato leaf sauce, pistou and pesto 178–80

pickles: pickled cherries 132

quick pickled onions 207

piña colada, gorse flower 108

pine nuts: mulberry cranachan 171–2

pineapple juice: The Rupert Holmes 108

pistou: tomato leaf sauce, pistou and pesto 178–80

plums: late summer fruit panzanella 175–6

porridge, New Year 14

potatoes: Bonnington tortilla 159–61

pan haggerty 217

potato and celeriac boulangère 57–9

rainy summer day pea and tarragon soup 151

twice baked potatoes with rosemary creamed leeks and smoked paprika 211–12

pumpkin seeds: pesto 178–80

Q

quince: Japanese quince jelly with star anise and white pepper 275–6

R

radicchio: salsify and radicchio gratin 262

radishes: fennel, rhubarb and radish coleslaw with elderflower dressing 46–7

rainy summer day pea and tarragon soup 151

rhubarb: double ginger rhubarb 41–3

fennel, rhubarb and radish coleslaw with elderflower dressing 46–7

rhubarb and lovage gimlet 94

rice: broad bean leaf and lemon risotto 110–12

rose-scented geranium leaves: herb sugar 254–5

herb syrup 255

rose sugar: hazelnut and rose cake 257

rosemary: tomato and rosemary soup 195–6

twice baked potatoes with rosemary creamed leeks and smoked paprika 211–12

rum: gorse flower rum 106

The Rupert Holmes 108
Seville orange spiced
  rum 28
Seville orange wintry
  mojito 28
runner beans: fresh
  tomato, runner bean
  and tarragon pasta
  186–9
The Rupert Holmes 108

S
sage: cauliflower and sage
  soup 23
pan haggerty 217
salads: cherry chana
  chaaty salad 189
fig, watercress and
  burrata salad with
  honey and fennel
  dressing 206
late summer fruit
  panzanella 175–6
salsify and radicchio
  gratin 262
sauce gribiche 85–6
asparagus and sauce
  gribiche on toast 86
seeds: New Year porridge
  14
sprouting broccoli,
  asparagus and spring
  flower gratin 90
sweet cicely apricots,
  yoghurt and mugolio
  125–6
Seville oranges: Seville
  orange bitters 26–7
Seville orange spiced
  rum 28
Seville orange wintry
  mojito 28
shakshuka, early summer
  135–7
shichimi togarashi 215
pan haggerty 217
shrub, gooseberry and
  elderflower 126–9
gooseberry and
  elderflower shrub
  G&T 129
smoked paprika, twice
  baked potatoes with

rosemary creamed
  leeks and 211–12
sorbet, strawberry 144
soups: cauliflower and
  sage soup 23
rainy summer day pea
  and tarragon soup 151
squash harira soup
  230–2
squash, leek and
  chestnut soup 245–7
tomato and rosemary
  soup 195–6
spice mixes: Chinese five
  spice 222–3
lebkuchengewürz 270
shichimi togarashi 215
spiced rum: Seville orange
  28
spring onions (scallions):
  asparagus and spring
  onion frittata 80
vignarola 121–3
sprouting broccoli,
  asparagus and spring
  flower gratin 90
squash: squash and
  celeriac fesanjan 251–2
squash cranachan 233
squash curd 232–3
squash harira soup
  230–2
squash, leek and
  chestnut soup 245–7
star anise: Japanese quince
  jelly with star anise
  and white pepper
  275–6
stew, chard, celery, butter
  bean and tarragon
  35–7
strawberries: gooseberry
  and strawberry Eton
  mess 143–4
strawberry sorbet 144
sugar, herb 254–5
a summer Tom Collins
  148
sweet cicely apricots,
  yoghurt and mugolio
  125–6
sweet potatoes: pan
  haggerty 217

syrups: fig leaf syrup 154
gorse flower syrup 106
herb syrup 255

T
tahini: baba ganoush 166
hummus 168
tarragon: celery and
  tarragon pesto 35–7
chard, celery, butter
  bean and tarragon
  stew with celery and
  tarragon pesto 35–7
fresh tomato, runner
  bean and tarragon
  pasta 186–9
rainy summer day pea
  and tarragon soup 151
Tom Collins, a summer
  148
tomato juice: Bloody Mary
  181
tomato leaf sauce, pistou
  and pesto 178–80
tomatoes on toast with
  tomato leaf pistou
  180–1
tomatoes: cherry chana
  chaaty salad 189
Devon spiced beans 238
early summer
  shakshuka 135–7
fresh tomato, runner
  bean and tarragon
  pasta 186–9
squash harira soup
  230–2
tomato and rosemary
  soup 195–6
tomatoes on toast with
  tomato leaf pistou
  180–1
tonic: gooseberry and
  elderflower shrub
  G&T 129
tortilla, Bonnington
  159–61
twice baked potatoes with
  rosemary creamed
  leeks and smoked
  paprika 211–12

V
vermouth: elderflower
  martini 115
mulberry martini 172
vignarola 121–3
vinegar, honeyed
  blackberry 203
vodka: blackberry allorino
  74
Bloody Mary 181
hazelnut vodka 248
Seville orange bitters
  26–7

W
walnuts: sprouting
  broccoli, asparagus
  and spring flower
  gratin 90
squash and celeriac
  fesanjan 251–2
watercress: fig, watercress
  and burrata salad
  with honey and fennel
  dressing 206
whisky, blackberry 201
wild garlic: green goddess
  dressing 64
wild garlic flowers:
  sprouting broccoli,
  asparagus and spring
  flower gratin 90
Wonka's allorino 73

Y
yoghurt: green goddess
  dressing 64
sweet cicely apricots,
  yoghurt and mugolio
  125–6

Acknowledgements

I'm delighted that only my name is on the front cover rather than the collection of brilliant, creative people who've lent their energy to making this book what it is. Firstly, to everyone who followed *Abundance* in weekly instalments at markdiacono.substack.com – thank you: your sharing of stories, comments, encouragement and love really made such a huge difference. To Harriet Webster, an editor with such great touch and wisdom, as well as being the best company, thank you. It's always such a pleasure. Huge thanks to the Quadrille team and those supporting: Sarah Lavelle for seeing the magic and having me as part of your wonderful family; Katherine Case, Gemma Hayden and Sarah Fisher for your design brilliance; Laura Willis and Laura Eldridge in marketing; Clare Sayer, copy editor; Sarah Epton, proofreader; Vanessa Bird, indexer; Martina Georgieva, production; Ruth Tewkesbury and Sabina Maharjan in publicity. Carolyn Gavin, thank you so much for the glorious cover painting that so captures the spirit of the book. As ever, a huge thank you to my agent Caroline Michel at PFD, for your lively support, enthusiasm and wisdom. To Laura Creyke at Mark Hutchinson Management – thank you so much for your creative, lively PR and marvellous company. To Laura, Dave and the gang in Rincon for the sanity-saving coffee and company. To Harris (aka Shitbag, Stinko, etc.), thank you for keeping me company on so many walks and making me stop more often than I might, which is always a good idea. Thank you Candida and Nell for eating, walking, and listening to the birds with me, and giving it all a point.

About the author

Mark Diacono is lucky enough to spend most of his time eating, growing, writing and talking about food. He has written several award-winning books, including *A Year at Otter Farm* and *A Taste of the Unexpected* (which both won Food Book of the Year for André Simon and the Guild of Food Writers, respectively), *Sour* (which was Food Book of the Year 2019 in *The Sunday Times* and *Daily Mail*, and nominated for a James Beard Award), *Herb* and *Spice*. Known for growing everything from Szechuan pepper to pecans to Asian pears, Mark's refreshing approach to growing and eating has done much to inspire a new generation to grow some of what they eat. Mark has a monthly column in *The Sunday Times* and writes regularly for a range of publications including *The Telegraph*, *Delicious*, and *Country Life*; his features have appeared in *The Observer*, *Guardian*, *National Geographic*, and others. He runs the Cafe Murano Book Club with Angela Hartnett, and speaks and demos at food festivals around the UK. Mark originally wrote *Abundance* as a serialisation on his Substack, 'Mark Diacono's Garden to Table', for which he won the Garden Media Guild Digital Gardening Writer Award 2024.

An extra thank you

When I started writing this book live in weekly instalments, thousands of people read along. Not only is it a joy to know they are there, their comments, stories, emails and more also reassure, challenge and alter my thinking. It has been perhaps the most rewarding period of my writing life. Every one of them helped create this book, and it continues at **markdiacono.substack.com**. Here are some of those I'd like to thank.

Ada Mournian
Adam Jackson
Adrian Bennett
Adrian Garside
Alex Keerie
Alexina Anatole
Alison Bell
Alistair Thompson
Amela Marin
Andrea Burden
Andrew Fisher Tomlin
Andrew O'Brien
Angela Clutton
Anita Oakes
Anna Carr Griffiths
Anna Rose Bing
Anna Taylor
Anna Thomson
Annabel Nourse
Anne Adams
Anne Black
Anne Stobart
Annie Graves
Annie Sutcliffe
Anthony O'Toole
Antonia Bolingbroke-
  Kent
Barrie Thompson
Bee Lilyjones
Belinda Davies
Bob Pennycook
Caroline Cockrell
Caroline Emmet
Cassie Harman
Charlotte Berger
Chris Wood
Chris Yates
Christella George
Christie Dietz
Christine Arnold

Christine Jackson
Christine Kimpton
Christine McFadden
Ciara Ohartghaile
Claire 'Auntie
  Bulgaria' Ruston
Claire Lindow
Clare Heal
Clare Huggett
Clare Southall
Dame Gladys Botticelli
Danielle Ellis
Darron Dupré
Deborah Durrant
Deborah Vass
Diana Heyer
Diana Morgan
Elisa Rathje
Elisabeth Luard
Ellie Thompson
Ewa Opalinska
  Shephard
Fiona Bird
Frances Rawson
Gabi Smallbone
Gaby and Hans Wieland
Gill Bourbage
Gillian Hill
Giulia Scarpaleggia
Hannah Bienias
Harriet Brown
Hattie Ajderian
Heather Joyce
Heather Noad
Helen Gordon
Helen Lorimer
Helen Sturgess
Helen Thompson
Ian Gillett
Isa Carr Griffiths

Jack McNulty
James Alexander-Sinclair
Jan Fullwood
Jane Carlton Smith
Jane Measures
Jennifer Earle
Johannah Randall
Johnnie Peter-Hoblyn
Jo Fairley and
  Craig Sams
JoJo Thomson
Jo Thompson
Joy Roscoe
Julie Giles
Julie Ives
Julie Mitchell
Julie Zayour
Kate Roxburgh
Katherine Knaust
Katrina Coyle
Katy Grech
Kelly Reed
Kris McKeown
Laetitia Maklouf
Laura Fricker
Laura Wilde
Lauri Lawrence
Lev Parikian
Lisa McLean
Liv Sleator
Lizzie Wingfield
Lynne Kennedy
Maddy Stimpson
Maggie Haynes
Maggie Sinclair
Marjan Bartlett-Freriks
Mark Leach
Mark Thomas
Martyn Chilton
Matt Alder

Max Brearley
Melanie J. Johnson
Miriam Kennedy
Molly Williams
Nicky Richmond
Patricia Gray
Penny and Steve Machin
Peter Chapman
Pippa Martlew
Rhiannon Morris
Ronnie Bendall
Rose Whitehouse
Rosie Cubbin
Rull Orchard
Sada Ray
Sam Siddorn
Sarah Anatole
Sasha Dorey
Sharon Amos
Simone LeBoff
Sophia Shirley-Beavan
Sophie Morris
Stephanie Hafferty
Stuart Robinson
Sue Currie
Sue Hunter
Sue Linfield
Sue Llewellyn
Sue Vickers-Thompson
Tamara Verhagen
Tamlyn de Nobrega
Tara Wigley
Teresa Lynch
Terry Becher
Tim Hewitt
Verity and Anthony
Viv Scott
Wendy Shillam
Yvonne Ryan

Quadrille, Penguin Random House UK,
One Embassy Gardens, 8 Viaduct Gardens,
London SW11 7BW

Quadrille Publishing Limited is part of
the Penguin Random House group of
companies whose addresses can be found
at global.penguinrandomhouse.com

Penguin
Random House
UK

Published by Quadrille in 2025

www.penguin.co.uk

A CIP catalogue record for this book is
available from the British Library

ISBN 978 1 83783 056 5
10 9 8 7 6 5 4 3 2 1

Managing Director Sarah Lavelle
Project Editor Harriet Webster
Copy Editor Clare Sayer
Senior Designer Gemma Hayden
Designer Sarah Fisher
Cover Artist Carolyn Gavin
Photographer Mark Diacono
Food Stylist Mark Diacono
Production Director Stephen Lang
Production Controller Martina Georgieva

Colour reproduction by F1

Printed in China by C&C Offset Printing Co., Ltd.

The authorised representative in the EEA is
Penguin Random House Ireland, Morrison
Chambers, 32 Nassau Street, Dublin
D02 YH68.

MIX
Paper | Supporting
responsible forestry
FSC® C018179
FSC
www.fsc.org

Cover illustration and design by
Carolyn Gavin. Instagram: @carolynj

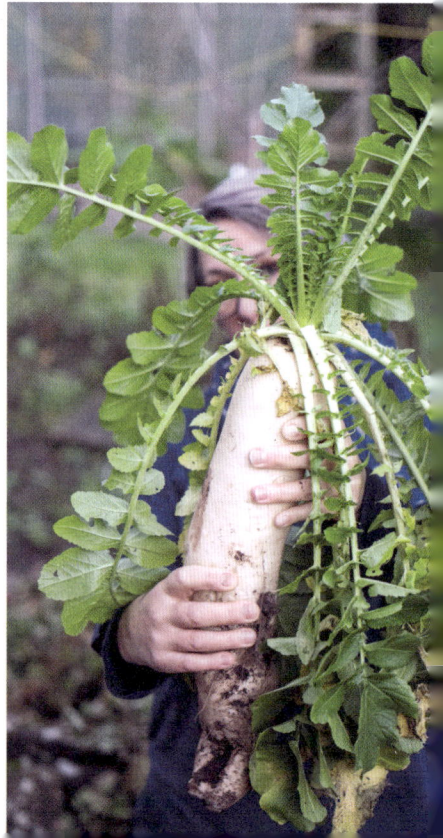